AA to Z

AA to Z

Addictionary to the 12-Step Culture

Christopher Cavanaugh

Main Street Books
DOUBLEDAY
New York London Toronto Sydney Auckland

A MAIN STREET BOOK
PUBLISHED BY DOUBLEDAY
a division of Bantam Doubleday Dell Publishing Group, Inc.
1540 Broadway, New York, New York 10036

Library of Congress Cataloging-in-Publication Data

Cavanaugh, Christopher.
AA to Z: addictionary to the 12-step culture / Christopher Cavanaugh.
p. cm.
1. Drug addicts—Dictionaries. 2. Recovering addicts—Dictionaries. 3. Alcoholics—Dictionaries. 4. Twelve-step programs—Dictionaries. 5. English language—Dictionaries.
I. Title.
HV5804.C38 1998
616.86′03′03—dc21 97-25139
CIP

ISBN 0-385-48340-6

Printed in the United States of America
March 1998
First Edition

10 9 8 7 6 5 4 3 2 1

In memory of my brother, John Andrew Cavanaugh,
and my father, John Daniel Cavanaugh

For Gail, Maggie, and Cooper, my three greatest loves

AA to Z

The 12 Steps of Alcoholics Anonymous

1. We admitted we were powerless over alcohol—that our lives had become unmanageable.

2. Came to believe that a power greater than ourselves could restore us to sanity.

3. Made a decision to turn our will and our lives over to the care of God *as we understood Him.*

4. Made a searching and fearless moral inventory of ourselves.

5. Admitted to God, to ourselves, and to another human being the exact nature of our wrongs.

6. Were entirely ready to have God remove all these defects of character.

7. Humbly asked Him to remove our shortcomings.

8. Made a list of all persons we had harmed and became willing to make amends to them all.

9. Made direct amends to such people wherever possible, except when to do so would injure them or others.

10. Continued to take personal inventory and when we were wrong promptly admitted it.

11. Sought through prayer and meditation to improve our conscious contact with God *as we understood Him,* praying only for knowledge of His will for us and the power to carry that out.

12. Having had a spiritual awakening as the result of these steps, we tried to carry this message to alcoholics and to practice these principles in all our affairs.

The 12 Traditions of Alcoholics Anonymous

1. Our common welfare should come first; personal recovery depends on A.A. unity.

2. For our group purpose, there is but one ultimate authority—a loving God as He may express Himself in our group conscience. Our leaders are but trusted servants; they do not govern.

3. The only requirement for A.A. membership is a desire to stop drinking.

4. Each group should be autonomous except in matters affecting other groups or A.A. as a whole.

5. Each group has but one primary purpose—to carry its message to the alcoholic who still suffers.

6. An A.A. group ought never endorse, finance, or lend the A.A. name to any related facility or outside enterprise, lest problems of money, property, and prestige divert us from our primary purpose.

7. Every group ought to be fully self-supporting, declining outside contributions.

8. Alcoholics Anonymous should remain forever nonprofessional, but our service centers may employ special workers.

9. A.A., as such, ought never be organized; but we may create service boards or committees directly responsible to those they serve.

10. Alcoholics Anonymous has no opinion on outside issues; hence the A.A. name ought never be drawn into public controversy.

11. Our public relations policy is based on attraction rather than promotion; we need always maintain personal anonymity at the level of press, radio, and films.

12. Anonymity is the spiritual foundation of all our traditions, ever reminding us to place principles before personalities.

Introduction

Throughout the world today, over two million alcoholics and hundreds of thousands of drug addicts, compulsive overeaters, sex addicts, compulsive gamblers, codependents, and other addicts abstain from their addiction, having found a new life by practicing the 12-Step program of recovery developed by Alcoholics Anonymous. They work each of the 12 Steps and engage in the fellowship of their programs.

Not too many years ago, addicts of all sorts had no means of recovery. That was until the mid-1930s. At that time, an American alcoholic named Rowland H. traveled to Switzerland to undergo treatment from Dr. Carl Jung. Rowland spent a year there, and Dr. Jung helped him to see his inner life and to recognize things that triggered his drinking. Rowland came back to the United States certain that he knew so much about himself that he would never drink again. He was mistaken. In a short time, he got drunk and ended up trapped in the nightmare of alcoholism as badly as ever.

Rowland went back to see Dr. Jung. This time Dr. Jung told him the basic truth—to stop drinking Rowland would have to have himself locked up or hire a bodyguard. Jung also told him that if he kept drinking he would probably die. Rowland asked him if there was any grain of hope. Jung told

Rowland that in rare cases, people have had a profound spiritual experience that enabled them to stop drinking. These people had huge personality displacements, let go of their old set of beliefs and behaviors, and picked up an entirely new set. Jung also told Rowland that he had been trying to elicit such an experience in him.

Rowland felt that he could accomplish this conversion because he was a man of church and faith. Jung told him that church and faith were not enough. Rowland came back to the States and sought out a new way of life with God at the center. He joined the Oxford movement, an evangelical Christian group modeled after the early church. He joined and never drank again.

Rowland had a drinking buddy named Ebby T. Ebby got himself in trouble with drinking, so much so that he faced jail if his drinking continued. A hopeless alcoholic, Ebby ended up facing a judge once again. Rowland and two other Oxfordians interceded and convinced the judge to release Ebby into their custody. Ebby joined the Oxford movement and went to New York to serve at the Calvary Mission with Dr. Sam Shoemaker, the head of the Oxford movement in America. Ebby had a drinking buddy from childhood who now lived in New York. His name was Bill W.

Ebby knew that Bill was having trouble in his work and trouble with drinking, so when he got to New York he contacted Bill with hope of helping him. Bill was delighted to hear from an old pal. Bill figured that they could drink together, reminisce, and recapture the laughter of their youth. He also welcomed having someone to drink with, because his loneliness and isolation were painful. When Ebby showed up at the door, Bill didn't recognize him. He looked healthy, and sober! Bill invited Ebby in for a drink but Ebby refused, telling Bill that he no longer drank and that he had found religion. Bill thought to himself, Well, he's gone from being a boozing crackpot to a religious crackpot.

Despite his disappointment, Bill invited Ebby in to chat anyway. While they talked, Ebby told Bill about the six steps of the Oxford movement:

1. Surrender to a God of your understanding
2. Examination of one's conscience
3. Confession of character defects to another
4. Practice of making amends when someone has been injured
5. Meditation and prayer
6. Quiet time, following meditation and prayer

These steps were a planned course of action, meant to bring about a personality change, just as Dr. Jung had prescribed for Rowland H.

Bill didn't believe in any of it, and he kept right on drinking that night and for several more days. In December of 1934 he ended up in Towns Hospital for another round of treatment under the care of Dr. Silkworth. Bill overheard Dr. Silkworth give his wife, Lois, the same prognosis that Dr. Jung had given Rowland—that unless Bill locked himself up he'd die. He had no control whatsoever over drinking. When Bill heard that, he paid attention. He also remembered what Ebby had told him. Bill struggled with the idea of a higher power, but he struggled more with the thought of insanity or death. He cried out, "If there is a God, let him show himself." At that moment Bill had an instantaneous form of the spiritual experience that is vital for an alcoholic to stop drinking. Bill describes the experience in his story in the Big Book.

Bill left the hospital and became involved with the Oxford group in New York. In Bill, three vital understandings necessary for recovery from addiction came together: he learned from Dr. Silkworth that alcoholism is a disease composed of an obsession and an allergy; he knew he was hopeless unless he maintained spiritual enlightenment; and he found a means to maintain his spirit—the Oxford group.

Bill set out on a mission to save other drunks. He embarked on the quest for about six months, with no luck sobering up anyone else. He discussed this with Dr. Silkworth. Silkworth told Bill that the other drunks probably thought he was crazy because he kept telling them all about his spiritual experience and they didn't have a clue what he was talking about. He advised Bill to hit them with the cold, hard facts first—tell them about your own drinking, and then teach them about the allergy and the obsession.

Shortly thereafter, Bill traveled to Akron, Ohio, in hopes of taking over a company. The deal fell through. Bill was low on cash and depressed about his business failure. On a Saturday afternoon he stood in the lobby of the Mayflower Hotel in Akron. Across the way sat the hotel lounge. Bill could hear the music, the sound of ice in the glasses, and the laughter. His alcoholic side thought that in the bar he could make a few friends and relax after his horrible setback. His sober side didn't want to go back to the old life and felt panicky. Bill knew that he never wanted a drink when he actively tried to help another alcoholic quit drinking, so he went to the church directory in the lobby to search for a local pastor who could help him find another drunk to work with. He told the pastors about his affiliation with the Oxford group, and one pastor referred Bill to Henrietta Seiberling, an Oxford member who lived in Akron.

Through Henrietta, Bill arranged to meet with Dr. Bob, a surgeon swimming in it. Dr. Bob wasn't too high on the idea of meeting this stranger, but he liked Henrietta and agreed to meet with Bill. Dr. Bob said he could spare no more than fifteen minutes. Well, the two men met on a Sunday afternoon at about five and they talked until eleven that night. Dr. Bob was the first other alcoholic to whom Bill had given the whole picture—allergy, obsession, hopelessness, and recovery through a spiritual experience. Dr. Bob had his last drink on June 10, 1935—this is the founding date of Alcoholics Anonymous.

Bill and Dr. Bob thought they should try the same approach with another drunk to see if it really worked. They found Bill D. in a local hospital, and gave him the whole picture too. Then they found another drunk, and another drunk, and another drunk, both in New York and in Akron. Soon there were approximately forty sober alcoholics.

By now they knew that their program worked, but they were still members of the Oxford movement, and there was some trouble there. Nonalcoholic members of the Oxford groups weren't sure that alcoholics were worth much of their time. Alcoholics in the movement felt that the "four absolutes" of the Oxford movement—absolute honesty, absolute usefulness, absolute purity, and absolute love—were unattainable goals and felt it better to seek progress rather than perfection. So for this reason, and because it was very difficult to protect the anonymity of alcoholics in an evangelical movement, Bill and his followers decided to split off from the Oxford groups.

Now that they were on their own they needed a vehicle to carry the message to the millions of alcoholics who still suffered. They thought of hiring missionaries, building hospitals, and writing a book. The last was the only affordable method. Bill, with the help of the collective membership in New York and Akron, wrote most of the book *Alcoholics Anonymous* (affectionately known as "the Big Book") in 1938. When the book came out, the new movement used the title as the name for their fellowship. Another small group began in Cleveland, and in 1939 total membership in Akron, Cleveland, and New York stood at 100. Membership in Cleveland boomed later that year when an article and positive editorial about A.A. appeared in the *Cleveland Plain Dealer*. Membership in that city surged from 20 members to 500.

The fledgling society struggled to recruit new members for another couple years—until 1941. That year *The Saturday Evening Post* ran an article by Jack Alexander about the A.A. fellowship and how so many formerly hopeless alcoholics were now living happy, productive, and sober lives. The year that article appeared, total membership in A.A. went from 2,000 to 6,000.

A.A. continued to grow, and by 1950 had approximately 100,000 members. People with other addictions, drugs for example, also sought the help of A.A. This created tension within the groups because some alcoholic members thought that A.A. should be just for alcoholics, while others felt that anyone who could benefit from practicing the 12 Steps should be welcome and supported. It turned out that other addicts had trouble within A.A. too, because they could not identify with alcoholics the way they could identify with other addicts.

As a result, several other 12-Step programs began to appear. Al-Anon, which grew up around A.A., officially began in 1951. Narcotics Anonymous began in 1953, and was the first fellowship of addicts that borrowed A.A.'s 12 Steps. Gamblers Anonymous was formed in 1957. These new programs are wholly separate from A.A., but share the traditions and steps, and the basic 12-Step way of life. Worldwide today, there are over 3 million people who practice a 12-Step recovery program.

It's been proven by the experience of all these programs that it doesn't matter if you drink it, smoke it, shoot it, snort it, jerk it, control it, obsess about it, spend it, or wager it—if it makes you stupid and if it's killing you, the 12 Steps offer a way out.

While recovering people find delight in their newfound freedom, they come to the programs, and stay, for serious reasons—the alternative being jail, insanity, or death. That's why these fellowships are so strong and continue to grow. Nothing else can claim the success rate for helping addicts find recovery. The programs work through sharing of one's self, finding a higher power, love, continuous fellowship, mutual support. Practice of these principles offers much more than freedom from addiction—it changes people and totally transforms them into new beings. For the first time in their lives, recovering people know that they fit in somewhere and that everything is going to be OK.

Through the years, the people who live a 12-Step life have formed a unique culture, with a language, history, and set of customs all its own. This book attempts to document that culture.

Through research, reading 12-Step literature, attending open meetings of several fellowships, and in-depth interviews with thirteen members of various 12-Step programs, I have assembled the basic language, history, lore, and humor of the 12-Step culture. The thirteen contributors have been the key.

I have attempted to give generic explanations for terms and slogans, but the contributors have shared what these phrases mean to them—from their hearts.

We start with Jack's story. Jack has experienced so many addictions and compulsions—and has been able to find recovery from them—that his entire story is included. I think that each of you will be able to identify with at least a part of Jack's struggles and successes. Following Jack's story you'll find short profiles of the twelve other contributors who helped me define the language of the culture. I selected 12-Steppers from a wide variety of programs and from a wide variety of locations. You'll probably recognize some of them (even if you've never met them).

The bulk of the book is a dictionary for 12-Steppers—it consists of the words that make up the language of the heart. It is not meant to be a self-help book. Rather I hope it will entertain and teach you about the wide variety of experiences within the 12-Step culture. I also hope it will instill pride in each of you, because you are a vital part of a movement that has helped millions find solutions to their problems, and continues to provide recovery for suffering addicts every day. 12-Step groups offer a unique environment. They are the only place I've ever been where anyone who needs to talk can talk, and when one person talks everyone else listens—and cares about what's being said. There's also a belief within the programs that people are inherently good and can be trusted.

In the appendices you'll find a bibliography of recovery-related publications, a listing of 12-Step program addresses, and a rundown of recovery sources on the Internet.

While many of the main offices of the fellowships provided invaluable help to me in this project, this book does not speak for any of the fellowships. The opinions and definitions are purely those of the contributors and myself. If you read something here that does not sit well with your program, as you understand it, I urge you to disregard it. Follow the suggestion of my friends from Al-Anon—*take what you like and leave the rest.*

Happy recovery!

Jack's Story

Jack had his twenty-year sobriety anniversary two days before he told this story.

My story begins in 1955, when I was born into a family with a mother in therapy trying to find out why her marriage was failing. My parents separated in 1958, when I was three. My younger brother, the fifth son, was born that year, coming into the world with a mother and father completing a divorce. The last two kids born to this family started out with two parents who didn't love each other. My mother was an alcoholic, and I became one myself. As I got sober and began to look back, I found that much of the hole in my soul came from my initiation to the world.

Because of the healing that I've done, I now have compassion for my mother, rather than anger. I did a lot of rage work in therapy. I confronted her and even though she didn't break or crack at all, something's totally different for me. I wouldn't want her to live here full-time, but I can talk to her today. The wildest time in my recovery was finding out the truth.

When I was five, I was living with my mother. My dad was a successful businessman and he was out traveling the world.

My mother drank heavily at this time, trying to deal with the stress of a failed marriage and trying to raise five boys alone. I really don't remember my mother at all from my early childhood. I remember most other people, but not her. She was drinking and housekeepers took care of my brothers and me.

I do remember that in 1962 my mother broke her back in a car accident. She was out driving after drinking a quart of vodka, and rolled her car. A judge decided that she was not capable of taking care of us, so the five of us went to live with our father.

I didn't know until twenty-five years later that this is what happened. Before then, my mother had told me that she had been out to get pizza for our dinner and that she came upon two cars drag-racing and got forced off the road. As a man, I found out that one of our housekeepers testified that my mother had drunk a quart of vodka that day. When I found this out, it created a tremendous rage in me. My mother lied to me for years, even when she was a sober A.A., just so she could protect herself from her own pain. I never heard the truth about my own childhood until I did my own investigation. My mother's story had always been that she crashed trying to save herself, and that my father used the accident to his advantage and took us away from her. He had the money to pay for good lawyers, or so the story went. She wanted us to think that she was a victim. In truth, she was a full-blown alcoholic.

She never told me the stories about her falling asleep in bed with cigarettes. Or about our neighbors going to the police chief to tell him to get the boys out of the house because my mother was going crazy again. One time she locked my oldest brother out of the house and he had to go next door for help. She never told me these things. She was always the victim and my father was a bastard. Instead, I wish she would have said, "I was a drunk and you guys are lucky you got through it the way I was behaving." My mother still doesn't admit any of it. She's just celebrated twenty-seven years of sobriety, and has built up greater protection from her pain now than ever before.

On the other hand, when my dad and I had a talk about all this ACOA (Adult Children of Alcoholics) stuff, thirty years later, he looked me right in the eye and said, "Jack, it was horrible what you kids had to go through. It was really a shame, and no kid should live like that." That was all he said, but with a couple of sentences he created a bridge between his heart and mine. Today we are great friends. My mother and I are about as close as you can get without having an emotional relationship.

In 1962 we all moved to my father's and the five boys began to split up. My three older brothers went to boarding school, because my dad couldn't take care of all five of us. Each older brother went to a different school. My father hired a woman to take care of my younger brother and me. He remarried, but his new wife got leukemia and died after only fourteen months. Between the ages of eight and fourteen, it was just my little brother Tommy and me most of the time.

I was an angry kid and I took out much of my frustration on Tommy. When I was eleven or twelve my dad started knocking me around, some physical stuff, but mostly verbal. He'd come home and just tear me up, calling me "a stupid son of a bitch," or "you asshole, what's the matter with you screwing up again." He had this loud, booming voice. Then he'd swat me across the head or back and send me to my room. It seemed like I'd be stuck in my room for the rest of the weekend, but then he'd be gone again.

I don't remember spending any intimate quiet time with my dad curled up watching TV, or reading, or anything. I lived in a military, disciplinarian atmosphere. I did spend some time with my father skiing and sailing. These were things he liked to do and I went along for the ride.

When I was about thirteen, my older brother came home to visit. He was living in Colorado and had gotten into drugs. He turned me on to my first drug, which was a hit of LSD. He sold me and my friend hits of acid for $15. Back then the drug sold for about $5, but he had found a couple of live ones and reeled us in.

Until the day of my first drug use, I had spent every day feeling weird. I had moved from place to place—by the time I was in ninth grade, I was in my tenth school. One year I had attended three different schools. For a couple of years my father had left my little brother and me with some woman in Vermont. We didn't live with him, and we didn't know where my mother was (turned out she was in and out of rehabs). Until the time I took that drug I felt as though I looked weird, I felt fearful, I felt like a little runt, I felt like every guy I looked at was cooler than me, I felt inadequate, and I was scared of girls. A typical alcoholic story of having the ISM before you pick up a drink or drug.

When that drug went into my system it did for me what it does for everyone who is a sitting duck for drug addiction and alcoholism. It gave me a feeling of pure contentment. Going to a party that night, I could talk to people and I felt like I fit in.

One thing led to another. I started smoking pot and taking pills, and I started getting lit up on booze. It became my little secret. I knew that a lot of kids were doing it too, because of peer pressure and things like that. But I knew it was my solace, my higher power. It made me feel like I could function in life. So I took to it like a magnet and tried to be wherever drugs and alcohol were found.

At the same time, I began to go through puberty. As with my older brothers, puberty brought out my anger, and again, I'd take it out on my little brother. By now, my father had married one of our baby-sitters (he was forty-four and she twenty-four), and she and I used to have fistfights on the kitchen floor. We'd fight all week and then my dad would come home on weekends and get the report. He'd then knock me around. Finally he told me I couldn't live with him anymore. I had the choice of going to boarding school or going to live with my mother.

The choice was pretty easy to make. My father was a tough disciplinarian. When I wasn't getting the physical abuse, I got verbal abuse. I was really scared of him all the time. My mother got sober in AA in 1966. So from then until 1971 we visited her for a weekend every six weeks or so. I began to get to know my mother during those years. I thought going to live with my mother would be heaven. She was a nondisciplinarian, and I knew she couldn't control me. When my father told me I could go and live with my mother, I was in alleluia land. So in 1971 I went to live with my mother. I was in ninth grade for the second time.

I did ninth grade three times and then I quit school. I was a bright young man, but I never went to class, so it was hard to pass. In my typical MO, I'd go out and party at night, stay out until 3 A.M., get out of bed around noon the next day, and go to one class in the afternoon. Usually shop class, where I wouldn't have to think too much. I could not sit through math or English, it was just too intense, especially if I wasn't high on something. I got suspended many times and finally in 1972 I quit.

My mother had no control over me. She'd tell me to come

home by midnight and I'd come in at four. She'd tell me to at least come home, and I'd just stay out all night. I think she decided to detach, meaning she knew she couldn't control me so she went on with her life. For her that meant helping other alcoholics get sober. In the meantime, I attempted to destroy myself.

I spent my teen years in the world of drugs and alcohol. I started shooting dope and used the needle for three years. For me that was better than any drinking or pills I had ever done because I could get the dope right into my bloodstream. My two favorites were heroin and cocaine, but I was sticking needles in my arm with drugs that I didn't even know the name of. My friends and I ripped off drugstores, taking the narcotics drawer and sticking syringes in morphine bottles, Demerol bottles, and codeine bottles. I had ten or fifteen holes in my arm—a pretty scary sight. I just loved the feeling and I didn't really care if I died. There were times when I'd be shooting dope and I'd think, I'm going to die if I shoot this. I'd shoot cocaine ten times in a half hour. I'd do some and five minutes later the rush is over and so you heat up some more in a spoon and shoot it over and over and over again. I'd think, My heart is going to freeze up, or I'd think, I might die on this one, but I'd do it anyway.

So for the three years when I was fifteen, sixteen, and seventeen I used mostly dope and pills. I found myself in the back of a police car often. The last time I was arrested, when I was seventeen, it was for armed robbery. I drove the car while two guys held up some kids at a college. My wife Janice, who was then my girlfriend, was in the front seat with me. The four of us got caught and arrested. Janice had just graduated from high school and was working at a bank as a teller. Her boss heard about it on the radio and she was fired. We all made statements and Janice got out of it. I went to jail for five days while awaiting trial with these other two guys. They were both about twenty years old and were both convicted felons already. My dad had lots of money and my lawyer said just follow me and I'll get you probation. That's what happened, I got five years probation. At the time I remember thinking that drugs were getting me in too much trouble and I was ending up in jail too often, so I decided to switch to alcohol.

I started drinking a lot and hanging out in bars. I believe I kicked the drug habit with alcohol. If I didn't drink, I think I would have gone into some pretty bad withdrawals. I put down the drugs and picked up a drink, which was just as good and allowed me to stay out of trouble. I also acted out my addiction by having sex with anonymous people and by masturbating to pornography. I was a cross-addicted person who couldn't stand to be with myself. I didn't care if it was getting high or having orgasms. Whatever made me feel good kept the fear and anxiety away. I was seriously dating Janice at the time, but I lied to her about my sexual conduct, and about my drinking.

A major event leading to my recovery happened when I was sixteen and strung out on drugs. I went to Colorado. The brother who had first turned me on to drugs had moved there. He'd had a very deep religious experience that straightened out his life. He became a born-again Christian. I remember him coming back to New York totally changed from the long-haired drug addict I had known. He now had short hair and a Bible under his arm, and he told everyone how the Lord helped him with every part of his life. I was intrigued by that.

I was hitchhiking across the country with a friend of mine, on the way to California. It was a way to pass the summer. We decided to stop in Denver and stay with my brother for a couple of days. He invited us to a prayer service and I went not knowing what to expect. I knew deep down that I was hurting badly and I knew that I had much trouble in my life. I'm not sure what happened that night—whether the minister gave a sermon that caught me, or it was the testimony of others about how God changed their life—but when they did the altar call at the end I went up. I went up to the altar and said a prayer asking God to come into my heart. A major transformation took place that night. I had a very profound spiritual experience, or in religious terms I felt the Holy Spirit. I remember going back to the pew, and my friend was freaking out. He said, "Man, what are you doing? You're going to ruin our whole trip." I said, "Buddy, something happened up there. I feel the presence of God. I've never felt this before."

When I woke up the next morning I didn't know whether to continue my trip with this guy or not. He asked me how I felt now, and I said, "Let's go get high." So I was back on the trail of getting high. But I had made a very honest, sincere plea to God to come into my life. Even though I continued to get high, my life changed from that day forward. For the next four years before I got sober, I had a presence of God in my life and a conscience. I had an awareness of my behavior and all the lying I was doing, and I developed a sense of guilt and shame. I think that the experience I had with God in Colorado was a major reason I got to A.A.

When I came into A.A. at twenty years old, I had been praying to God off and on for help. I told God I didn't know what to do, I told him I'm crazy, I'm suicidal, and asked him to please help me. I never paid attention to the idea that I might be an alcoholic or a drug addict. During those four years I would wake up feeling rotten with a hangover, feeling the guilt, and I'd promise God that it wouldn't happen again.

At five that evening, I'd be on my way to the deli to get a six-pack to get started for the night. I knew emotionally and spiritually that I couldn't go on this way anymore. I asked God repeatedly for help, and I ended up at an A.A. meeting.

The last two years were all alcohol. I really identify with the Big Book term "impending doom." That's what I felt over my head every day. I'd think, I'm going to die today, or, I'm going to kill myself today. I couldn't drink anymore because it was killing me, but I couldn't not drink because I couldn't stand being straight. I was in a state of desperation. I don't know how I held on as long as I did.

I considered suicide daily. I felt so alone, even in A.A. I was around many people and they all seemed to be doing fine, but I was in hiding. The secrets I tried to keep, the guilt and the shame, the knowledge that God wanted better for me, the moral code I kept but could not live up to, not being able to live the way I wanted to, not being able to live life as it was, all added up and made me think about suicide all the time.

I had my last drink on November 4, 1975. I had been to a couple of open A.A. meetings in September of 1975. I went to the early meetings because of a violent episode with Janice. I threw her down and tried to choke her, and I threw her up against a car. We were at a party and the more drunk I got, the more I thought I could drive. I had already lost my driver's license, but I told her to give me the keys, I'm driving. She said, You're drunk, you're not driving. So I ripped the keys out of her hands and she ran from me. She had never done that before. She had always grabbed me and told me to control myself. But she ran from me and I saw the look on her face. I thought to myself, I can't do this anymore.

I walked from there to a nearby bar and drank the rest of the night away. The next morning I woke up and remembered what had happened. I never had blackouts, and that may have helped me to get into recovery too. I remembered everything the next morning—the look on Janice's face, that physical abuse, everyone looking at us and me feeling they were thinking, How can Janice be with this guy? So that's when I went to my mother and asked her if she thought I could go to an A.A. meeting.

My mother asked me if I had a desire to stop drinking. I said yes, even though I still wasn't sure. I knew I was out of control. So I went to some meetings. About six weeks later, a friend of mine asked me if I wanted to go with him on a trip down south. Everyone in A.A. said that I shouldn't, but I did anyway. I said I'd be all right, I was only going for about ten days. I told my friend that I didn't drink, and that I didn't want to drink on the trip.

We got in the car and drove about twenty miles. We crossed a bridge that leads to New Jersey. When we got to the other side the compulsion hit me. We were on our way from New York to Florida. I freaked out and I sweated my way through New Jersey and Delaware. By the time we got to North Carolina I couldn't hold on any longer and I told him to pull over so we could get a six-pack. He said, "I thought you weren't drinking." I said, "Well, we're on vacation." I drank like crazy for two nights. The morning after the second night, I woke up and had my first beer at about eleven. I finished about half of it. I looked across the campsite and I saw a group of other kids drinking too. Something hit me that day. That was the day I truly felt I could not do it anymore. I put the half can of beer on the table and asked the guy if we could go home.

That was my last drink. It's the only time I can remember having only half a can of beer. Because I was a compulsive person and if I had one, I'd need sixteen. I'd go to parties and if the host had a couple of cases, I'd take a couple of six-packs and hide them in the bushes and go back to the party and drink what was left. I'd make sure I had extra if the party ran out.

That half can of beer was my bottom. I wrote a letter to God, which I had never done before, saying, "Dear God, I don't know what I'm going to do. I'll go back to A.A., but I'm not sure that's going to do it. If I don't get help there, I'm going to kill myself." I went to the meeting on a Sunday night. The guy leading the meeting was about twenty-one years old, and I was twenty. Bells were going off in my head as I listened to him and I went up to talk to him at the end. We went to my house afterward and talked for two or three hours, and he became my sponsor. I started going to meetings. I didn't hear about 90 in 90 in those days, but I bet I did it because I knew I had to go to be safe.

My first year, as each day passed, I got angrier and angrier that I couldn't drink anymore. I thought my life was over, and I hated feeling everything. I felt it wasn't fair because I was too young. On my first anniversary a celebration was planned for me, but I told my mother I wasn't going. She asked why not. I said I hated sobriety and I hated A.A. She told me she had invited Lois W. to come. (Lois is the wife of A.A.'s cofounder Bill W. She herself cofounded Al-Anon.) I said, "I don't give a shit about Lois W.! Who cares about Lois W.?" I didn't realize that eight years later when I had my baby son, she'd be there to hold him. Or that I'd go to her house to talk to her often and we'd become good friends. I went to my anniversary meeting, but it was a miserable night.

The first year was tough. It was really, really hard to stay sober. I think what kept me sober in the first year, maybe even the second year, was the first step. It didn't say we were alcoholic, it said we were powerless over alcohol and that our lives had become unmanageable. That's exactly what I felt sitting on that table in Florida. That's exactly what I felt when I wrote the letter to God. When I saw the words of the first step in A.A., I thought, Shit, I can't deny that. So for me to go pick up a drink again felt impossible because the jig was up. Jack, you've been found out. There's a label for what you are, whether you say you're alcoholic or not, you are powerless and unmanageable—and there's no denying it. To me, the first step is magical in the way it is written.

I admitted the first step to Janice and to my mother and to other people. It helped me to know that they were all pulling for me too.

I moseyed my way through the next couple of years, with the first three steps. I went to a step study group and got cornered by some steppies. They called me on not working the program hard enough and told me it was time to do step four. I had bullshitted my way through this group for six months by saying I had done the steps in my old group, but I never had. I never did an honest fourth and fifth step. Six different people got six different versions. I needed to truly bare my soul to someone.

When I did the fourth and fifth steps, I began my years in A.A. where I felt as though I belonged. I felt comfortable and I even liked A.A. That lasted about seven years, until I was ten years sober.

At ten years, life inside began to get pretty shitty. I was a young old-timer. I had a good job, a condo, I was married and had a son. People looked up to me. I sponsored several people, and others would call me asking my advice. I got off on this attention and adoration too much because I had never fixed any of the problems of my inadequacy or my feelings of inferiority. Helping people was my way to feel good about myself—it became my drug. If I wasn't helping someone, I couldn't feel good.

I never took the chance of not having all the A.A. people around. I was always helping people and sponsoring people. I drove to detoxes and rehabs to take down-and-out people to meetings. I helped everyone I could. People would pat me on the back and say, "Man, you're the greatest guy in the world."

I really wasn't in touch with all this until I was ten years sober and I realized I was doing all this because there was a major void in my life—a hole in my soul. I needed the pats on the back as much as I needed drugs. I remember running off to a meeting one night and Janice asking me, "Why are you going tonight? You just went last night." I answered, "Well, they need me." I remember hearing myself say that and wondering, Shouldn't I go for me?

During the time I was five to ten years sober, I got back into my sexual addictions with pornography. I was faithful to my wife, but I used pornography for my affairs. Masturbation fought off the feelings I had about myself with moments of exhilaration that were as strong as shooting dope or drinking a bottle of Jack Daniel's. It was also safe—I wouldn't drive my car off the road or beat up my wife. I got into obsessing about sexual stuff heavily and it was killing other parts of my life. I had guilt and shame about it too. Here I was, looked up to as this great A.A. guy, but I had all kinds of secrets. I put on the mask of what I thought people wanted me to be at A.A., and it worked. I played the role and acted as if I was happy. It wasn't on purpose, but I did it to survive.

From years five to ten, I went to step meetings and Big Book meetings only. I got very good at quoting A.A. literature and pulling sentences out and expounding on the meaning of it all. It seemed as if people were really digging what I talked about, and they thought it great that I was married and had kids and a good job. Here's a guy who's a success—thirty years old, ten years sober, makes good money, has a big house. I want to be like Jack when I get sober.

In reality, I hadn't dealt with other addictions and I had tremendously low self-esteem and felt inadequate. I thought if others knew the real me, they wouldn't want me around. That's what shame is for me. John Bradshaw says that rather than feeling I made mistakes, I felt I was a mistake. Until I got into therapy and started working with some of those old voices—what my dad and baby-sitters used to say, and the fact that no one ever helped me when I was a kid, or hugged and kissed me—I never dealt with the deeper issues.

The problem with talking about it in A.A. is that people say, "Oh come on, get over that shit. That was in the past." The truth is if you don't deal with the stuff that really happened to you, I'm convinced you'll have other addictions and a secret life going on. I felt deep down inside that I was no good, that I was inadequate and if people really knew me they'd flee. Since I've worked in therapy and in ACOA, and since I've really gotten to know a higher power that loves me no matter what, that stuff feels totally gone.

I found ACOA through a guy I sponsored. He had gone to an ACOA meeting and he told me about it. I made some snide remark like "What's that bullshit, ACOA?" I was around twelve years sober and not in a good frame of mind. It seemed like everything was coming to a halt, the whole world was crumbling. I remember being in really bad shape, and I was trying to fake that I was doing OK. At a meeting this guy next to me, who had two months sober, nudged me and said, "The meeting's almost over, aren't you going to share? You always sound so good." My mind said, "I know I sound good. I'm really good at sounding good, but I'm not good. Where do I go? Who's there for me?" I felt like a failure because I didn't know how to get sobriety right.

I don't remember if it was that night or the next night, but my sponsee started talking about ACOA again. He gave me something called a laundry list to look at. It felt ten times as overwhelming as when I first read the twelve questions of A.A. In A.A. the questions take this approach: Do you ever drink in the morning? Yes. Do you drink to feel more comfortable around other people? Yes. Do you ever lose time at your job because of your drinking? Yes.

Those are pretty cut and dried questions, but they don't go to your soul the way the ACOA laundry list does. Statements like: "We judge ourselves without mercy." "We're either super responsible or super irresponsible." I was always super responsible, always on time, never could say no. So I said to my friend, "Now wait a minute, they talk about this stuff at ACOA meetings?" He said yes.

I remember going home and telling Janice that I was bottoming out emotionally. She knew it from my behavior. I told her I was going to go to an ACOA group. I couldn't decide if I was ready for ACOA or ready for a gun, but I figured I might be able to get some help.

I walked into my first meeting, twelve years sober, supposedly knowing all there is to know about 12-Step recovery. I sat there like a kid in nursery school and said, "I don't know anything, help me." I couldn't believe I was at that point, but I also couldn't believe that there was another 12-Step program that cared for another part of your world—your secret world, and your shame world. I could learn to deal with my inner person, and my family of origin. I felt overwhelmed by this meeting, my hope renewed.

In A.A. I couldn't put my feelings about this, my inner life, into words, and even if I could I felt I couldn't talk about it. In ACOA people talked about all the stuff I had kept hidden. This Tuesday night ACOA meeting became my rock for the next two or three years. I had finally found a place where they verbalized all that I felt before I found drugs and alcohol and after I quit drugs and alcohol.

In A.A. they figure if you've gotten five years sober you're doing OK no matter what you're going through. In ACOA, if you have twenty years sober and say you're falling apart, they say that's cool. I felt I could be me for the very first time.

After about six months in ACOA, I got into a therapy group that had some people in A.A. and some that were not. That was a really great three years for me. I did a couple of week-long sessions at the Carin Center, dealing with codependency issues. It involved intense family of origin work and sculpture work, grieving, crying, swinging bats at pillows, rage work, all that stuff. A whole new world opened up for me about healing the inner person. I learned that recovery isn't just about getting my family back and getting my job back—it's about getting me back.

Bob Earle is one of my favorite writers on the program. He said, "There was only one thing missing after seventeen years of sobriety—me! I had no self. When I went into therapy and ACOA, I found my self—a self that I could love, a self that I didn't have to run from, a self that I could look at in the mirror."

I started practicing what John Bradshaw calls "uncovery." In A.A. you recover; in ACOA and therapy you uncover. The uncovery leads to discovery. I've done much uncovery work that helps me discover me, a self that I really like. I still struggle with things, I get down sometimes, and I get discouraged. But it's a whole different world. As I go through those feelings I now say, "Well, I'm supposed to be feeling these things." If I'm not supposed to be feeling what I'm feeling I can turn it over to my higher power or share it with another person. I don't beat myself up for having uncomfortable feelings. With just A.A. I often thought that if I felt bad, I was bad.

I heard a Bob Earle tape in which he described his shame as being like a little boiling pot of sewage deep down in his heart. No one else could see it but it was always there, boiling away. That's what shame is. Deep inside you don't have one good feeling about yourself. Deep down thinking that no one could love me, not even God.

I'm much different now. I began to see my new life five years ago when I was teaching a Sunday school class. A man who sat in on the class came up to me afterward, stuck his hand out, and said, "You know, you're a really neat guy." It's the first time I ever remember not looking at the ground when someone said something nice to me. I could never make eye contact. I remember looking this guy right in the eye and saying, "Thank you."

I remember flying leaving that church, thinking I never did that before. I used to hear that and say, deep down, well, you don't know me, man, I'm just an act.

I had to go back, relive and feel all the information I got as a kid, and then reprogram it. If I didn't become conscious of the programming I'd received, I'd have lived with it all my life. When I came out of the world of drugs and alcohol, I was still living with the bad programming.

I still have feelings. I moved from New York to Florida last year and I felt tremendous loss, of friends, of places where I'd meditate. I went through terrible grief, to the point where I wanted to die. But there's a healthy place in me today. That's where I get a little angry at A.A. They let people hang around too long. There should be a rule that after five years you should enter therapy automatically. If you're still smoking cigarettes and drinking lots of coffee and eating cookies and say you're doing fine—don't do any of it for two weeks and see if you're doing fine. I quit smoking after eight years. Then I started watching what I ate. I started to feel, and it hurt.

Contributor Profiles

Audrey M.
From New York
A member of Alcoholics Anonymous
Sober 5 years

Audrey drank to blackout as early as age thirteen. She had the terrible experience of having a mother who committed suicide and a father who blamed her for not watching over her mother better. Audrey also had an air of sophistication and beauty that enabled her to find a rich husband who could take care of her and give her the life she thought she wanted.

Despite her outer life, Audrey had a hole in her soul that no one could fill. She drank and drugged her way through life even though she had children to care for. When she lost an infant daughter, Audrey's dark life took over completely. She and her husband split up. She tried the geographical cure many times and ended up living with one of her sons in a shack.

She decided to kill herself with drugs and alcohol and boarded herself in a room to die. After being in the room for three days she woke up out of a blackout and looked outside to try to see what time of day it was. It was night, and she spotted the full moon. The beauty and the peace of the night sky gave Audrey a sense of peace. She saw herself in the reflection on the window and recognized for the first time that she was not the woman of grace and beauty she pictured herself to be. She saw that she was just a drunk. Audrey heard her son crying and praying to God to help him because he couldn't take care of her anymore. At that moment she knew she'd hit bottom and needed help.

Cooper P.
From Oklahoma
A member of Alcoholics Anonymous and Al-Anon
Sober 8 years

Cooper had tried beer as a young teen but didn't really take to it. When he got to college he tried scotch, straight up, at a fraternity party. From there he never wanted the party to stop. On one hand Cooper had many successes. He made the cut as a Navy Seal, and served in that elite fighting unit during the early sixties. When he left the Navy, Harvard Divinity School accepted him as a student. After graduation, Cooper went through what he describes as twenty years of grayness. He had a wife and children, but his life centered around getting drunk. Eventually as he hit bottom, his family intervened and talked him into going to treatment. He's been sober since.

Cooper works an Al-Anon program too, because he has family members who are also alcoholics. A.A. helps him deal with booze, and Al-Anon helps him deal with personalities.

Greg K.
From Connecticut
A member of Alcoholics Anonymous
Sober 3 years

It's taken Greg about seven years to put together three continuous years of sobriety. This time around, Greg's recovery has centered on service to other alcoholics. Greg thinks this is what's enabled him to stay sober, along with his faith in God and good sponsorship.

Sobriety has been good to Greg. While he struggled with work and relationships as an active alcoholic, he now enjoys a challenging job and has a new love in his life. In just three years his life has completely changed.

Greg loves A.A., and at least once a day he thanks God for the fellowship.

Jim C.
From Iowa
A member of Alcoholics Anonymous and Overeaters Anonymous
Sober 20 years, practicing OA for 10 years

Jim's problems began as a sex addict in his teen years. If he were around certain women, alone, they would end up having sex. To control those urges as a married man, Jim turned to alcohol and food. The weight he carried protected him from his uncontrollable sexual urges. Two addictions controlled one.

When he got sober Jim initially lost some weight, but food remained a problem. He entered OA and started to control his eating. Then sex became a problem again—especially with certain women in OA.

Today Jim successfully practices the 12 Steps to recover from all his addictive behavior. He now abstains from alcohol and compulsive eating, and he avoids being alone with women who trigger his sex addiction.

Jim N.
From Iowa
A member of Gamblers Anonymous
Abstinent from gambling for 2 years

Jim started gambling on the golf course. As he got better and better at golf, he began to play against better golfers. These golfers played for money and Jim joined in. His new golf friends also bet on sports, and introduced Jim to a local bookie. Soon Jim became obsessed with sports betting, and he also began to lose large sums of money. In desperation he stole money from his company and lost it too. He became hopeless and tried killing himself twice. After the second failed attempt, he woke up to the fact that he needed help and checked himself into a rehab. Jim takes abstinence seriously. He won't even play games for free food at fast-food restaurants.

Marilyn L.
From Iowa
A member of Al-Anon for 30 years

Marilyn struggled in Al-Anon for the first nine years. She had a sponsor who practically had to drag her to the one meeting a month held in her city. In the early years of her recovery she tried to control Ted's drinking, even going as far as sneaking Antabuse into his food. She experienced years of pain and failure trying to keep Ted sober, but nothing worked.

Bewildered, she expressed her fear and dread to a friend who was a member of A.A. and he told her that she had to face the fact that Ted might not ever get sober. He told her to ask herself, "Do you want to live like this for the rest of your life?" She said no, and he told her she'd have to turn Ted over to the care of God.

Marilyn did this, and has had the rewards of Al-Anon recovery for over twenty years. (Incidentally, Ted went into rehab three months after Marilyn turned him over to God.)

Marilyn had the honor of speaking at the 65th Anniversary Convention of A.A. and Al-Anon in San Diego in 1995.

Mary C.
From Idaho
A member of Narcotics Anonymous
Clean 10 years

Mary describes herself as a garbage head. She started out at age nine with alcohol, and went on to use whatever she could get hold of to get high. Mary went to her first meeting after getting out of jail. She was alone at her parents' house and knew she was in trouble. She tried to call an old friend who she knew had gotten sober. She tried calling him several times but the phone was busy for two hours. Finally she made a bargain with God—she'd try to call for help one more time, but if the phone was busy she'd jump out the window to kill herself. She tried once more and her friend picked up. (He had been on the phone with his sponsor.) Mary started in A.A. but found NA a better match for her.

Her recovery has been a process of staying clean and trying

to rid herself of the toxic shame she can feel at times. She tries to be honest about her feelings with herself and with her friends, saying, "It's the secrets that will take me back to drinking and drugging."

Nicole G.
From California
A member of Debtors Anonymous
Abstinent from debt for 6 years

Nicole went around for years carrying resentments toward her employer, her husband, her friends. She felt less than all of them and tried to cover up her feelings by overspending and buying herself things that she thought would make her feel better. Her spending got out of control to the point where she could not pay her rent or bills. She found Debtors Anonymous and now owes no one. As a spiritual exercise, Nicole keeps it that way too: she pays the doctor at the time of the visit, buys things only when she can afford to pay cash, and will go without a soda at work rather than borrow change from a coworker.

Ron H.
From New Mexico
A member of Narcotics Anonymous
Clean 15 years

Ron came from a family of addicts, and actually entered 12-Step programs through Al-Anon. His sister, a recovering person, saw that Ron's life sucked and tried to 12-Step him. Ron resisted, insisting that he wasn't that bad. She said, "Well, Dad's an alcoholic, our brother's an alcoholic, I'm an alcoholic, maybe you should go to Al-Anon." This didn't sound too bad, so Ron went to an Al-Anon meeting. His sister was right, he did need Al-Anon, but when he heard other Al-Anons share about the unmanageable lives of their alcoholics, he knew he was on the wrong side of the fence. Reluctantly he went to A.A. and found the door to his own recovery.

A couple of guys at an A.A. meeting asked Ron if he wanted to go to the best meeting in town. It turned out to be an NA meeting. Ron was more of a pothead, and could identify more with NA's emphasis on addiction, rather than alcohol. He saw the NA meeting as being like A.A., except you could swear and if you talked about drugs no one would glare at you. So for Ron, NA it was.

Ted L.
From Iowa
A member of Alcoholics Anonymous
Sober 21 years

Ted has a history of trouble with employers and with the law. First he lost his job as a bellboy because the hotel found out about his bootlegging operation. Later he landed in jail for punching a cop after being pulled over for reckless driving. His wife, Marilyn, found out about his arrest in the morning paper.

Ted's bottom came when Marilyn stopped enabling him and gave him over to God. (Marilyn, a member of Al-Anon, also shares in this book.) Marilyn told Ted that she loved him, but that he was on his own. If clients called for him, she'd tell them where to find him—even if they had to call him at a bar. For three months Marilyn let Ted do as he pleased, and "cook in his own grease." Ted finally submitted to the reality of his disease and asked a neighbor who was an

A.A. member to help him. Ted went to treatment that day and has been sober since.

Tim K.
From Ohio
A member of Alcoholics Anonymous and Overeaters Anonymous
Sober 7 years, practicing OA for 2 years

Tim, a physician, got in trouble with alcohol and narcotics to the point where he was suspended by the state medical board, and had to go on five years probation. His journey in recovery has gone from a heavy concentration on A.A. during the early years, to today where he puts his emphasis on treating his compulsive eating in OA. Tim also works on inner child issues, trying to experience the pain and grief that he never let himself feel.

Vinny B.
From New York
A member of Sexual Compulsives Anonymous
Abstinent from compulsive sex for 5 years

Vinny used sex to escape his feelings of inadequacy and insecurity for over ten years. He found places like men's rooms, parking garages, and bars where he could have sex with other men. He led a secret life for all those years, knowing something was wrong but never knowing how to control himself. He went to a gay and lesbian center for treatment for a sexually transmitted disease, and while there saw a bulletin for the SCA fellowship. Vinny thought, Wow, compulsive sex, that sounds like me. He went to a meeting and read the characteristics. It blew him away to see that others had the same problem.

After struggling with the program for a year, Vinny hit bottom when he angered two of his best friends. He'd brought a man back to the summer house they shared, saw that his housemates were still up, so went to the backyard with the man. The housemates heard them and called the police. It all got straightened out, but Vinny saw then how unmanageable his life had become. He began to work the program with a new fervor and has found great success in SCA.

The Addictionary

How to read the Addictionary:

- Terms are arranged in alphabetical order. Members of 12-Step programs are listed by their first names, so look for Bill W. under B. Civilians are listed by their last name, so look for William James under J.
- Words in small caps are defined elsewhere in the book.
- For consistency the word *addict* is used generically to refer to everyone who practices a 12-Step program. After all, alcoholics are addicted to alcohol, and compulsive overeaters are addicted to food.
- The words "clean" and "sober" are used interchangeably.
- Direct quotes from contributors are in *italic* type.
- Profiles of the contributors can be found in the previous section.

A

AA. Acronym for Attitude Adjustment, or Altered Alcoholics.

A.A. Is for Alcoholics. Although the A.A. 12-Step program can help many people with many problems, the A.A. fellowship exists for the primary purpose of helping alcoholics get and stay sober. While there are many open A.A. meetings that welcome people with other addictions, drug addicts, overeaters, codependents, gamblers, and others have found it best to start and use programs specifically for their problems. It seems to work best when members see themselves clearly in the other people. In A.A., a minority of members don't want to hear anyone share anything that's not about alcohol. Fortunately, there are other fellowships like NA, OA, GA, and Al-Anon to go to. *I remember sitting in an A.A. meeting on a Saturday morning. I'd O.D.'d on peanut butter sandwiches the night before and had as bad a hangover as I'd ever had on martinis. I shared about it. There was an old warhorse who sat across from me and when it got to be her turn she looked at me and said, "Honey, we got real problems here." I felt shamed. But at that meeting also was a guy who went to A.A. to supplement his OA program. He was one of the few guys I'd ever met from OA. His name was Jerry. Jerry came up to me and said, "Have you ever heard of OA?"* JIM C.

Abstinence. The practice of avoiding a substance or behavior. In A.A. this is simple (but not easy): members do not take alcohol into their bodies. In other programs such as OA and SCA the practice becomes more complicated, because no one stops eating or having sex. In these programs, members develop a recovery plan, and abstain from any addictive substance or behavior that's not on the plan. For example, a member of OA may have a recovery plan that allows her to eat three moderate, healthy meals per day. She'll avoid all other eating. *Abstinence used to be described in a two-part way: something you did, and something that happened. Abstinence for me is a state of mind.*

When I have what I call God-given abstinence, there's a clarity of thinking that's not available to me when I'm drinking, eating, or acting out sexually. OA used to suggest abstinence, but now there's a food plan. You follow a food plan that's different for everybody. For me a food plan is one that enables me to be in that frame of mind, my God-given abstinence. I do not have that all the time, maybe just ten percent of the time. When I compare OA to A.A. I see that it's impossible to attain complete abstinence in OA. If you slip, what's important is that you admit it honestly and then you keep going. In A.A. it's more devastating. You start over, saying, "I got one day." JIM C.

I smoke cigarettes and I drink coffee. I don't change my clean date every time I smoke a cigarette. If I did I'd have to look at how chocolate affects me, how food affects me, and how sex affects me. I have to keep it simple. I know what brought me here and I know what I need to not do, and what I need to do to stay clean. Medications are widely discussed in the NA fellowship, and probably always will be as long as people continue to search. If someone has to have surgery, I'm not going to say they shouldn't go under. We have people who are schizophrenic. I'm not going to tell them to stop taking their medication. I've seen schizophrenics in recovery who feel guilty for taking medicine and stop taking it. Guess where they're at in a week if they're still alive, they're using. I can't say don't take medicine in recovery. I do know that it takes a hypervigilance and a hyperdiligence in recovery to work the steps and connect with your sponsor and do the things you know you have to do. Like any other choice in my life, I need to take a fearless and searching inventory, pray, and be honest with others. MARY

In DA, abstinence means not taking on any unsecured debt. I won't borrow money from anybody now. If I don't have the money to buy a soda at work, I go without. I won't borrow the money from a coworker. I also do things like bring the cash to pay when I go to the doctor. It's a great feeling when I look at my calendar and all my bills are paid and I know I don't owe anyone. NICOLE

For me abstinence is avoiding any mind-altering drug, alcohol, and any form of gambling. I don't place sports bets, go to casinos, go to the track, participate in office pools, play the lottery, or play games at fast-food restaurants where you pull a tab and see if you've won a free drink. I abstain from drugs and alcohol because there is a strong chance for cross-addiction. It's very easy for us to substitute one addiction for another. JIM N.

Abuse. Using a substance, behavior, or other person in a destructive manner. A person who has a beer after a softball game is not abusing alcohol; a person who sneaks off from the bench to down a pint of whiskey and then drinks ten beers after the game is abusing alcohol.

Acceptance. Many 12-Steppers believe that acceptance is the answer to all their problems, that nothing happens in God's world that is not meant to happen, and that working on acceptance is the key to serenity. A recovering person accepts their addiction, the fact that they are sick, and the program as a means for a better life. See PAGE 449.

Act As If. A slogan often told to NEWCOMERS who feel crazy, or want to use. They're told to act as if they were sane, or not wanting to use, because all you can really change for the moment is your actions, not your feelings. It's also useful for OLD-TIMERS, because they can lose their serenity too.

Action. Any behavior that helps a 12-Stepper move toward a goal, be it SERVICE to others or personal growth.

Act Your Way into Right Thinking. A therapeutic breakthrough for the 12-Step program of recovery. Psychotherapists try to help people understand their feelings and get them out in the open, and generally try to help people think straight so they can begin to act right. 12-Steppers take the opposite approach: they try to get newcomers to act right. When a new person begins to act right, their feelings become exposed to them because they're not covering them up with substances and behaviors. Then they can deal with their feelings and begin to grow.

Addict. A person who abuses a substance or behavior, and cannot stop without the help of a higher power. Some characteristics include:

- A high sensitivity to bodily changes induced by substances
- Wide mood swings
- Bad judgment
- Obsessional thinking and compulsive behavior
- Isolation
- Denial

In NA there's a saying that the problem is being an addict, the solution is drugs. It's an irony, but as I look back on my life I see that the drugs didn't cause the problem. The problem was my low self-esteem and my deteriorating ability to be social. RON

An Addict Is an Addict Is an Addict. 1. What a SPONSOR tells a PIGEON when the pigeon thinks they can still use substances other than their drug of choice. 2. The idea that the substances aren't the problem, addiction is the problem, and an addict will use whatever they can get to change how they feel. *I bought my favorite aftershave at a department store and got a free gift of a specially formulated shaving cream. I tried it, and found that the shaving cream had a topical anesthetic that made my face tingly and numb. It really felt great. My first thought was that I should try rubbing the shaving cream all over my body to get an even greater sensation. I guess I'll always be an addict.* COOPER

Addict Waiting to Happen. This is how many recovering people describe their fearful, neurotic childhood. *I always seemed to have a curiosity about sex, and I can remember as a young child watching TV and there were certain erotic images that excited me. I don't know if I felt sexually stimulated, but I felt some excitement. At the same time, I felt shame over that. The images could be anything from Captain Kirk being bare-chested, or sexual innuendos on* Love American Style. *VINNY*

Advice. NEWCOMERS hate it, and OLD-TIMERS know better than to give it, so it's strictly a passion of the sophomoric 12-Stepper. A better approach to helping someone is to listen to them, and then share your own EXPERIENCE, STRENGTH, AND HOPE. SUGGESTIONS replace advice.

Affirmations. Short, positive statements one makes to oneself in an effort to change thought patterns. Recovering people need to change how they think about themselves if they want to find self-esteem and serenity. With this recovery tool, the 12-Stepper repeatedly reads and/or recites positive messages. Affirmations can be found in countless books for recovering people, or they can be written by individuals to suit their own needs. Examples:

- My higher power has released me from my addiction. I know that miracles can happen for me
- Today I seek to become a man that I admire

- I will care for all of me, even the parts I don't like
- Other people like me when I let them know me

Aftercare. Follow-up care for people newly out of rehab. Groups of patients return once or twice a week to the rehab, or other designated meeting place, and help each other through the struggles of living a clean life. There is generally a professional facilitator present for these sessions. Aftercare is not a substitute for 12-Step meetings. Successful recoverees typically attend both meetings and aftercare.

Akron, Ohio. Where the 12-Step movement began. BILL W. traveled to Akron on a business trip and there met DR. BOB. Together they tried to stay sober by helping one another and other alcoholics. The first call they made was to BILL D. in an Akron hospital. Bill D. and Dr. Bob started Akron's Group No. 1, the world's first 12-Step group. The group still meets on Wednesday nights at eight at the First United Church of Christ, located at Work Drive and West Exchange. Other points of interest in Akron: the Gatehouse, where Bill W. and Dr. Bob first talked, and the Mayflower Hotel lobby, where Bill made the crucial decision to look for another drunk to help.

Al-Anon. The Al-Anon Family Groups are a fellowship of relatives and friends of alcoholics. Al-Anons consider alcoholism to be a family disease, which they too suffer. In their fellowship they try to follow the 12 Steps to spiritual awakening. Al-Anon started as coffee and cake groups for the wives of alcoholics in A.A. Soon these wives started to see that they too had many of the same problems as the alcoholics and decided to use the 12 Steps in their own lives. In 1951, a small number of these groups organized into the Al-Anon Family Groups, through the leadership of

LOIS W. and ANNE B. Their PRIMARY PURPOSE is to help families of alcoholics through the 12 Steps and 12 Traditions of ALCOHOLICS ANONYMOUS. Al-Anon welcomes all who have been exposed to a relative's or friend's alcoholism, whether the alcoholic is still drinking or not. Many members have not lived with an active alcoholic for years, but still embrace the recovery offered by Al-Anon. It's a lifesaver for those who still live with an active alcoholic.

Alano Clubs. Privately owned clubhouses, usually purchased and supported by a group of recovering people. The clubs serve to provide a safe place for recovering addicts and alcoholics to have fellowship with others. The clubhouses are often rented to 12-Step groups for meetings and social events. This is a way to work around the tradition that 12-Step groups not own property.

Alateen. A part of the AL-ANON Family Groups that helps teenagers recover from the effects of living with an alcoholic, usually a parent. Alateen was started in California by Bob M., with the help of LOIS W. The groups operate much the same as Al-Anon, with members sharing their EXPERIENCE, STRENGTH, AND HOPE with each other. SPONSORS, adult members of Al-Anon, assist each group. An Alateen member is a full member of Al-Anon.

Alcoholic. 1. A person addicted to alcohol. 2. An egomaniac with an inferiority complex.

The Alcoholic. Generic term used by Al-Anons when they refer to the alcoholic(s) in their life. It encourages members to keep the focus on themselves and it fosters identification among members. Preferred to My Husband, or My Mother, or My Son. *"Well," my sister said, "you know Dad's an alcoholic, our brother's an alcoholic, I'm an alcoholic. Maybe you should go to Al-Anon." So I could deal with this approach, I went to Al-Anon. The topic of* *the first meeting I went to was the Seventh Step—humbly asking him to remove our shortcomings. I knew sitting in that meeting that there was something fundamentally wrong with my sitting in a meeting with these Al-Anons. They talked about themselves, but when I heard stories about the behavior of "the alcoholics" I immediately realized that I was on the wrong side of the fence. Being in a family of alcoholics, I did belong there. But the primary concern was about my life being out of control and I knew it—I heard it in that Al-Anon meeting.* RON

Alcoholic Foundation. The early name for what is now the GENERAL SERVICE BOARD of Alcoholics Anonymous. A.A. changed the name because the word "Foundation" invoked the image of charity, paternalism, and big money. A.A. wished to avoid all three.

ALCOHOLICS. Acronym for A Life Centered On Helping Others Live Completely Sober.

Alcoholics Anonymous. The granddaddy of all 12-Step programs, it's a society of men and women whose primary purpose is to stay sober and help other alcoholics to find sobriety. The fellowship began in 1935 when BILL W. found himself alone in AKRON, OHIO, on a Saturday afternoon having just experienced a business disaster. Standing in the hotel lobby, the sounds of the nearby lounge enticed him. Inside he could find relief and friendship. Panic overwhelmed him—he had not had a drop of booze in the last three months. He had to talk to someone, someone who would understand. Bill had found a singular solution to his years of pain and bewilderment as an alcoholic: if he tried to help another alcoholic, he would stay sober himself.

Bill found the local church directory and called the ministers hoping they could help him find another alcoholic to talk to. After much effort, he found DR. BOB, a local surgeon and hopeless drunk. Dr. Bob's wife arranged a meeting for the next day. Although Dr. Bob agreed to talk to the stranger for only fifteen minutes, the meeting that began at five that evening did not end until eleven.

Bill helped Dr. Bob as no relative, pastor, or physician could, because he knew the drinking game and Dr. Bob trusted what he said as true. Dr. Bob was the first other alcoholic to try the help-another-alcoholic approach. It worked! Together, to insure their sobriety, the two men set out to help others. That's how Alcoholics Anonymous began.

Over 2 million alcoholics are sober today because of that chance meeting over sixty years ago. Hundreds of thousands of drug addicts, gamblers, overeaters, codependents, and other addicts have found recovery in programs modeled after A.A.

A.A.'s growth over the years:

YEAR	NUMBER OF MEMBERS
1935	2
1939	100
1940	2,000
1941	6,000
1950	100,000
1998	2,000,000

Outsiders have had this to say about A.A.: "America's unique contribution to the history of spirituality." *Richard Rohr, O.F.M.* "The greatest spiritual movement of the twentieth century." *Keith Miller*

Jack Alexander. A hard-nosed journalist who reluctantly took an assignment from the *Saturday Evening Post* to write an article about A.A. He spent a month with A.A. members, both day and night. His emphatically positive article on the movement appeared in the March 1941 issue of the magazine. In response to the article, A.A. grew by four hundred percent in one year. The article is available in pamphlet form from A.A. World Services.

Allergy. An exaggerated or abnormal reaction to substances, situations, or physical states that are without similar effect on average individuals. WILLIAM DUNCAN SILKWORTH, M.D., who wrote "The Doctor's Opinion" in the Big Book, described the reaction of craving once booze enters an alcoholic's body as an allergy. This, combined with "an obsession of the mind" for the first drink, formed the foundation for the alcoholic's nightmare of addiction. The only solution, says Dr. Silkworth, is complete abstinence. *For me an allergy food is anything that I eat that causes me to want more and more and no matter how much I have I'm not satisfied.* *TIM*

Amends. The Ninth Step suggests ADDICTS attempt to repair their broken relationships by apologizing to those harmed, and by changing their behavior for the better toward these people. Just as amending a contract means to change it, the real point of Step Nine is to change the way you relate to others. *The part that made it hard for me was laying it on the line. Not just the apology, but the part where I said to people, "I'll do whatever it takes to make it right." I asked each person if there was something I could do now, not do, or do for the rest of my life to make it right. I really meant it and I was willing to take whatever consequences I faced. There were some situations where I thought that people might ask a lot of me. Most people responded very kindly, but there was one person who told me the best amend I could make would be to stay the hell out of her life.* *GREG*

Starting the repayment plan really helped me to see the rewards of making amends. NICOLE

Anne B. She helped her close friend and neighbor LOIS W. open and operate the first AL-ANON office at STEPPING STONES. They started the organization by writing to eighty-seven nonalcoholic family groups and individuals that sought registration with ALCOHOLICS ANONYMOUS.

Anne S. The wife of DR. BOB. She helped bring BILL W. and Dr. Bob together. She is also credited with reading the warning of James in the Bible that faith without works is dead to the early members of A.A. Anne counseled many family members before the existence of AL-ANON.

Anonymity. Keeping the names of members out of public view. It's called "the spiritual foundation of all our traditions." It began as a way to protect new members who were afraid that people in the community would find out about their addiction. As time went on, a new benefit became apparent: anonymity puts everyone on an equal level and cultivates humility. It discourages the drive for personal power, recognition, and profit; and it insures that no individual member speaks for any of the various fellowships.

ANONYMOUS. Acronym for Actions, Not Our Names, Yield Maintenance Of Unity and Service.

Antabuse (Disulfiram). Drug prescribed to alcoholics that discourages drinking by making the individual violently ill if a drink is taken. Conscious contact with a higher power works much better than Antabuse. *There was an insurance agent at my first meeting, and I'll never forget this, he talked about a drug that he was taking called Antabuse. He said it was keeping him from drinking. I thought I'd get some of this because I was pretty weak-kneed. I took Antabuse for the next nine years, trying to get my drinking* *under control. I never was able to. Truth be known, in those nine years I never got more than sixty days of continuous sobriety. I was red all the time. Antabuse made me very tired and it made my joints ache. I went to the doctor and told him how the Antabuse affected me and asked him for something to help me. He gave me a prescription for a diet pill. Boy, I'll tell you, those things really made me fly. I loved them. But then it got to the point where I couldn't sleep at night because the diet pills kept me awake. I went back to the doctor and he gave me a prescription for Equanil, which is a tranquilizer. Now I didn't know whether to get up, lie down, or take a shit. One day I was out in the backyard with foam coming out of my mouth, my system was so confused. I dropped both the diet pills and the tranquilizer and toughed it out on Antabuse. That is, until I turned my will over and began to practice the A.A. program.* TED

Anticipation High. Common experience, especially in cocaine addicts, where just the thought of buying drugs or the trip to the dealer will cause the addict to get high.

Area Committee. In the A.A. service structure, the Area Committee sits between the DISTRICT COMMITTEES and the GENERAL SERVICE CONFERENCE. Through its elected delegate, it keeps up with what's happening at A.A. World Services, and through its members it stays in touch with the local districts and groups. The committee's service responsibilities include helping groups find solutions to problems, active institutional work, providing public information, cooperating with the professional community, and insuring new groups and loners get the help they need.

As We Understand Him. The four words that have made spirituality accessible to hundreds of thousands of addicts who might otherwise have rejected 12-Step recovery.

Many, when active, had abandoned the concept of God. In 12-Step recovery they learn that they can have any conception of God they wish. In the Third Step, members make a decision to turn their will and life over to the care of God *as we understand Him*. The phrase is repeated in the Eleventh Step. Jimmy B., the self-proclaimed atheist who started A.A. in Philadelphia, is credited with pushing to have the phrase included in the steps. The phrase also gets members to think about what they believe their higher power to be, which facilitates spiritual growth.

Attitude of Gratitude. 1. What you're told to have when you bitch and moan about life in recovery. 2. How many recovering people describe their approach to life.

B

Back-Door Alcoholic. A person who comes into A.A. after first attending Al-Anon meetings. Often these people find the 12 Steps by trying to find relief from another's drinking, and then find enough honesty to admit to their own addiction.

Balance. A hard-to-reach goal for many 12-Steppers. Keeping recovery, work, family, and spirituality in the proper proportions is a lifetime struggle for most.

John Barleycorn. Booze personified, and the nickname for alcohol used by several storytellers in the Big Book. It comes from the 1787 poem "John Barleycorn" by Robert Burns, which says in part,

> John Barleycorn got up again,
> And sore surprised them all.

Bedford Hills, N.Y. The site of STEPPING STONES, the former home of Bill and Lois W.

The Best Way Out Is Through. A quote from Robert Frost used to explain to recovering people that they now need to allow themselves to experience the pains of life, and not try to hide anymore. ADDICTS tend to run away from grief, pain, shame, and guilt by using. This can mean that issues go unresolved for years. The programs teach people to talk out their anger, cry when sad, make amends when you hurt someone, and humbly ask God for help in living life.

Big Book: AKA *Alcoholics Anonymous.* Published by A.A. World Services in 1939. It is the basic text of A.A., and the most important document in the recovery movement. Written by Bill W. and other early members of A.A., it describes the principles of the program in the first 164 pages and devotes another 411 pages to personal stories of A.A. members. Despite two revisions of the book, the original first 164 pages remain just as first written. The program has worked too well for too many to risk changing anything. The book has sold over 15 million copies, which is true evidence of the power and reach of A.A. Many people in other 12-Step programs read the book for guidance and inspiration.

Big Meeting in the Sky. A 12-Stepper's vision of heaven.

Bill D. A.A. member number three. The first A.A. group, at AKRON, OHIO, began when BILL W. and DR. BOB convinced Bill D. that he too could find sobriety by applying the principles they had incorporated into their lives. His acceptance of the program, and his subsequent recovery, proved to Bill W. and Dr. Bob that their ideas worked. Akron's A.A. group number one started with Bill D. and Dr. Bob.

Bill W. Along with Dr. Bob, he cofounded Alcoholics Anonymous. He wrote the books *Alcoholics Anonymous, Twelve Steps and Twelve Traditions, Alcoholics Anonymous Comes of Age,* and *Twelve Concepts for World Ser-*

vice (part of the AA Service Manual). He also wrote numerous articles for the GRAPEVINE, and many of his writings are collected in the books *The Language of the Heart* and *As Bill Sees It.* His promotion of the program in the early days earned A.A. respect from government, churches, the media, business leaders, and society as a whole.

Bill is the most important figure in the history of the struggle against alcoholism and other addictions. While he did not invent any of the principles of recovery, he, with the help of other alcoholics, developed a proven program that enables addicts to live normal, useful, and serene lives.

He was born in East Dorset, Vermont, on November 26, 1895. Although he once had a promising career on Wall Street, alcoholism drove him to unemployment, illness, and despair. In late 1934, he learned from an old pal, EBBY T., that the OXFORD GROUPS were able to help some alcoholics find sobriety. When he landed in TOWNS HOSPITAL a month later for yet another treatment, Bill reflected on what Ebby had told him about the need for a spiritual realignment in order to recover. Bill then had an overwhelming spiritual experience, which included the insight that by helping other alcoholics, he could maintain his own sobriety. He went out and tried to help others find sobriety—with no success until he met DR. BOB in May 1935. Bill's success in helping Dr. Bob achieve sobriety led to the formation of A.A.

While he often spoke to medical, religious, and psychiatric societies, and he even testified in state and federal hearings on alcoholism, Bill declined all public honors.

Bill devoted much of his service to building a sound structure for the fellowship. In 1938 he established a board of trustees, and in the early 1950s he was instrumental in the building of the GENERAL SERVICE CONFERENCE.

When A.A. established the conference in 1955, Bill stepped down from active leadership.

Bill's Story appears in the Big Book, and there is a biographical film called *Hello My Name is Bill W.* often shown on television.

Bill died of pneumonia on January 24, 1971, in Miami Beach, Florida.

The fact that he had shortcomings makes Bill W. more important. He wasn't God, he was a human being with many failings. This to me says that a person who truly struggled with life was able to come up with the 12 Steps and all the rest of the great things he did. To say that he was a saint makes me think, well I'm not a saint so what does that have to do with me. Just like me, he had a lot of problems, yet he performed a great service for millions of people. I can identify with Bill and this gives me hope. When I hear people in A.A. say that it's just about not drinking, I recoil. I think about Bill and how he worked on his defects all his life. I prefer to follow his example. To me the 12 Steps are the way for me to become the way God intends me to be. It's a big job, but it feels wonderful to be in the process. TIM

The Bill W. Movement. A name Bill W. suggested for the BIG BOOK, his ego not completely deflated. Other members talked Bill out of it, quickly!

Binge Drinker. An alcoholic who does not drink every day, but who cannot keep from drinking regularly. A binge drinker's sprees can often last several days, and usually result in blackouts, illness, and deep regret.

Birds of a Feather Flock Together. Phrase used to describe the differing philosophies of various programs, and groups within the programs. Because there are so many different programs, and different kinds of groups, each individual can find a place where they feel comfortable. Some appreciate a hard-core Big Book thumping group, while others prefer a kinder, gentler approach. *I think 12-Step programs mirror factions of Christianity. We have fundamentalist groups and liberal groups and everything in between. I went to an A.A. meeting early on and a guy announced himself as an alcoholic and an addict. He was told he needed to go somewhere else to deal with that and that this meeting is only about alcoholism. That scared the hell out of me. Luckily I didn't say anything because I could have been sent out just as easily. Plus, they were all about fifty-to-seventy-year-old white men. I asked myself, "How did I get here?" Here I was in a T-shirt, jeans, hiking boots, and a leather jacket with all these old men. I felt like a black person at a KKK meeting. Just as there are people who interpret the Bible literally, each program has people who interpret their books and pamphlets literally.* MARY

Blackout. A period of amnesia, brought on by alcohol or another drug. An alcoholic, for example, can be drinking, be awake, and have interactions with others, but not remember any of it the next day. Sometimes alcoholics come out of blackouts still awake and don't remember what happened two minutes earlier.

Blame. People in 12-Step programs work at taking personal responsibility for their lives and actions. Placing blame on others becomes less and less important as spiritual renewal helps the recovering person see that everything that has happened needed to happen for life to be as it is today.

Many NEWCOMERS come into the program placing blame for their torn lives on parents, spouses, children, employers, friends, and anyone else they can think of. They're told: KEEP COMING BACK.

Blossom. An NBC television series about a young woman living with her divorced father and two brothers. In the show, Blossom's oldest brother, Anthony, is a drug addict and alcoholic recovering in A.A. The show offers an honest and humorous portrayal of a young man struggling with early recovery and the changes he has to make in his life. The show is now aired in syndicated reruns.

Bookend. To speak with another recovering person before and after taking a new, frightening, or stressful action. Recovering people talk through the situation first, take the action, and then afterward report how things went. *If I'm uncomfortable about something, say a business deal perhaps, I'll call another recovering person and talk things out. For example, someone once asked me if I would edit her book proposal. I said sure. Then she asked me how much I charge, and I told her I'd get back to her. I decided that she's a friend and I don't know how much money she has, so I'll charge her $25 an hour. Feeling uncomfortable, I called someone else in the program. She said, "Nicole, charge $50 an hour. Tell her $50. It's what you're worth." I was frightened, but I went ahead and called the writer, told her it would be $50 an hour, and she said that would be fine. I reported my success back to my program friend.*

Without the program I never would have called my friend and I would have charged $25 an hour, felt a resentment, and most likely would not have done a very good job. NICOLE

Born Alcoholic. While some believe they drank themselves into alcoholism, many A.A. members believe that their genetic makeup is such that they were alcoholic at birth. *Publicly, I felt resentment toward people who told me I needed help with my drinking. Inwardly I knew that they were right, and I knew it from the first time I took a drink.*

My mother told me that if your last name is K. and you take a drink, you're an alcoholic. So when I was eleven, I felt like I'd joined the alcoholic club. From the beginning I knew there was something wrong because once I started, I couldn't stop. GREG

Born of Necessity. Saying which describes the founding of 12-Step programs, and each individual's willingness to practice the program.

A.A. began because millions of people needed help with alcoholism. Drug addicts soon saw the power of A.A., but many could not identify with drinkers, so NA was born. This pattern continued, and now there are dozens of 12-Step programs that help people with all kinds of problems.

For individual addicts, the willingness to practice the program is born of the necessity to change, or else they die.

Bottle, Big House, or Box. Three options available to alcoholics who don't practice 12-Step recovery.

Bottom. The last straw for an addict. It's when life becomes so unmanageable that change becomes the only option to death or insanity. For some the bottom may be jail, others losing their families, and for some it's a desperate feeling of losing control of one's life. 12-Step programs teach that it's OK to start at the bottom and work your way up.

High Bottom. Reaching recovery with money, a job, and the support of family.

Low Bottom. Coming in off Skid Row.

I went to live with my brother, because I thought if I could get away from all my troubles, I'd stop drinking and drugging. The first night I was there I thought there was no way I could get through without a drink. So I went out to

the store and ended up drinking for three days. My brother was ashamed of me. My kids were ashamed of me.

My brother owned an apartment building and we stayed in one of his apartments. I had always had my own money and my own way with things, but now I didn't have anything. I couldn't ask my husband for anything because he didn't know where I was, and I couldn't ask my family because I had too much pride. So I went to welfare and that was the beginning of my bottoming out. About a year later I was living alone with my youngest son and I'd finally hit rock bottom. There was a knock on the door at about five that morning. It was an ex-roommate my son had called. "Audrey," she said, "you need help." I said, "You can't help me, I'm too much of a mess. Don't come in here, it smells awful in here. Go away." She did go away for a while. I heard my son crying on the back porch. He was praying to God to take him because he couldn't stand living with me anymore. He said, "I can't take care of her anymore." That's when I knew I needed help and I knew I'd hit my bottom. AUDREY

My bottom happened over a two-week period. I got to the point where I ran out of money and other resources. I thought that I was no good to anyone alive and that my only option was to die and make the death look like an accident so that my family would receive insurance money. No one would have to put up with my lies, or lack of money, or the other things I did to them. I didn't even feel I was a part of my family. I just did my own thing and the family fended for itself. If there was a Little League game or family function, they did it all without me.

I attempted suicide twice. The first time I tried to make it look like I accidentally electrocuted myself. My family

went out on an errand and I thought this would be a great time to kill myself. I stripped back some wires on a fixture in the garage. It turns out that 110 volts doesn't do much to you except give your arm a jingle. I learned something new that day.

About a week later I had stalled my bookie because I thought I could make another bet that would pay him off. That didn't work and I was deeper in debt. I was driving home and remembered that I had decided to run my car into a tree to kill myself. It was winter and getting dark, I think it was about 5 P.M., and I'd told my wife I'd be home at 5:30. As I drove home I scouted for a good accident site. I couldn't find any I really liked until I got pretty close to home. I spotted it and drove back around to the beginning of a straightaway that led to the tree.

I turned off the car and started thinking. It grew darker, and it got past 5:30. I started to make the run toward the tree, but someone pulled out of their driveway and slowed me down, so I circled the block again. I just circled the block for forty-five minutes, stopped and thought some more, and then started circling again. Eventually a yellow light on my dash came on warning me that I was running out of gas. I knew I had to do something quick. I stopped the car. At that moment I realized that I had to do something to change my life. I had to stand up to my problems and work it out because suicide was not the correct way to do things. That was my bottom. A couple days later I started treatment. JIM N.

Boundaries. Many addicts try to be all things to all people. This fosters resentment, and can lead to increased substance abuse or insanity. 12-Step recovery teaches addicts to say "no," to practice a selfish program, and to set limits with other people. Over time a recovering person learns personal boundaries. Keeping the boundaries guarded is a lifetime practice.

Box 459. The post office box number for the GENERAL SERVICE OFFICE of AA. Also the name of the General Service Office's bimonthly newsletter.

Box 658. AA post office box number in the early days. Located at the Church Street Annex Post Office in lower Manhattan, the box received thousands of frantic letters asking for help and information.

Bread Crumb. A small sign or occurrence placed by God to direct the spiritual paths of those who seek God. *At my first GA meeting there were three people I felt a linkage with. I wanted to show my appreciation to them for the help they gave me, so I gathered up some things we make at work to give to them as presents. I stopped at the last of the three's office to drop off the gift with no intention of taking up any of her time. She asked me if I had a few moments, I said sure. We talked for about a half hour, and then I left. I found out later that she had been having a very difficult day and had prayed for someone to talk to—there I was. It gives me a chill to think that my life had been arranged to be in this particular spot for this particular person.* JIM N.

Bridge Back to Life. For some 12-Steppers, the program is their life. For most, though, the program becomes the essential part of life that makes success with employment, family, friends, and other interests possible again. *In the early days of recovery, I hung around only with people in the program. That was very practical because if I was with those people, I would not use and that provided protection. Later, I began to internalize that protection and adapt my life to the steps, instead of vice versa. I did not need that external protection. Today, the program is the* *base of my life. I have interests outside NA and friends outside too. Most of the people I choose to be friends with may not be in a 12-Step program, but they all are trying to live an honest life. I tend to like to be around people who have similar interests, including spiritual interests, both in the fellowship and out.* MARY

The first year, my entire life revolved around A.A. On weekends I'd go to meetings Friday night, Saturday morning, Saturday night, and Sunday night. In between I'd go to coffee, play golf or softball with guys in A.A. It was exactly what I needed at the time. I loved going to A.A. every night. There's a guy in my area who calls A.A. a sufficient substitute. At ground zero, before sponsorship, before the steps, before a higher power that's what A.A. was for me. I went out drinking every night. A meeting every night was my substitute. I was still around alkies, I was still in a social setting, and it worked. Now I'm in a love relationship again. I try to balance A.A. with work and my relationships. Much of the time I'd rather be at a meeting, but I can't hide in A.A. But I feel good that I love the program so much that I miss going to so many meetings. I love hanging out with recovering alcoholics. GREG

Bring the Body, the Mind Will Follow. Suggestion made to NEWCOMERS who are too edgy or cynical to understand the program. It means to just keep coming to meetings, even if you think it's a waste of time. Eventually, you'll start to get it, if only by osmosis.

Buddy System. When two or more people in recovery decide to talk to each other often and go to meetings together. Unlike sponsorship, the parties usually have similar straight time. It's also useful to bring a 12-Step buddy to a stressful situation, like a party, wedding, or funeral. *Early*

on, I made friends with another newcomer who was just out of treatment. For months, he and I hit three or four meetings a day. We'd go to the ten o'clock meeting at a local restaurant, the noon meeting at the Presbyterian church, the two o'clock at the Lutheran church, and then go to an evening meeting. The last thing we'd do after coffee was arrange our meeting schedule for the next day. I'll be forever grateful for our time together because I got thoroughly immersed in the A.A. culture. COOPER

Business Meeting. A special meeting of a 12-Step group held to discuss the affairs of the group. Together, members make decisions on group leadership, allocations of funds, meeting format, and group conscience at these meetings. Many groups set apart special times for business meetings, so group issues don't interfere with their regular meetings. *Business meetings can get very intense in DA, especially if the topic is the treasury. People take it very seriously because dealing with the business part of life is the crux of the program. I've been in business meetings that became really uncomfortable, but I've seen that if you stick through it, everything gets resolved.* NICOLE

But for the Grace of God (or, There but for the grace of God go I). A program slogan that helps members remember that their recovery is not their doing, but their Higher Power's. OLD-TIMERS silently recite the slogan in their heads when a rough PIGEON rants at a meeting.

C

Came, Came to, Came to Believe. The process of spiritual awakening for many. You show up at meetings and stay clean; your head clears; and you see that what God has done for so many, God can do for you too. *When I first*

came in I had no notion that a God would want to have anything to do with me, period. But I remember thinking early on about the Second Step that hey, there's only 12 Steps, and they couldn't have written one twelfth of the program just for me. I must not be the only one. It gave me great hope. I don't know when, I don't know how, but I began to believe that I could believe. MARY

Came to Believe. A collection of stories by A.A. members, about how they found a HIGHER POWER that could solve their problems. A.A. World Services publishes the booklet.

Camel. A symbol of sobriety. *There's a poem that's associated with A.A. called "Dry as a Camel." It goes like this:*

The camel each day goes twice to his knees;
He picks up his load with the greatest of ease;
He goes through the day with his head held high;
And he stays for that day completely dry.

I have a camel pendant I wear around my neck, and I carry a medallion that has a camel on one side with the words "one day at a time" and the poem on the other. TED

Caretaker. Common term used in AL-ANON for a person who is obsessive and compulsive about fixing other's problems, at their own expense.

Carry the Message. Step Twelve suggests helping other addicts. Experience has shown that a recovering person can tell of their own experience, strength, and hope, but they cannot make the suffering addict hear or understand. Thus the slogan: Carry the message, not the alcoholic. *My sponsor used to tell me I needed to figure out the difference between carrying the message and spreading the disease.* COOPER

Chairperson. 1. Person who leads a 12-Step meeting. 2. A NEWCOMER elected (often railroaded) to set up the chairs for a 12-Step meeting.

Change. The transformation process for those in recovery, where one becomes a new person. It's never easy, yet seldom without value. Addicts spend years avoiding change when active, and years facing and accepting change in recovery. *It was an illusion that my problem had been drinking, I thought that when I stopped everything would be wonderful. I thought I didn't have to change, all I had to do was not drink. I came to realize that this is a living disease and that I have a problem with life.* COOPER

The most miraculous changes I've experienced, aside from not using, are the removal of anxiety and being comfortable in my own skin. I love the sense of being OK. MARY

Today I have clarity. I know how much money I have and how much money I have to pay in bills. I've paid off my creditors little by little. For one I paid $20 per month for three years. It was great when I finished off that debt. NICOLE

Change or Die. 1. Two choices for an active addict. 2. What a hard-core 12-Stepper tells a hard-core addict.

Chapter Five. In the BIG BOOK, Chapter Five is titled "HOW IT WORKS." Many A.A. meetings open with a reading of the first three pages of Chapter Five. The TWELVE STEPS of A.A. appear in Chapter Five.

Character Asset. 1. A personality trait that helps a 12-Stepper serve God and other people. 2. An item listed on the benefit side of a Fourth Step inventory ledger.

Character Defect. 1. A personality trait that prevents a 12-Stepper from serving God and other people. 2. An item listed on the liability side of a Fourth Step inventory ledger. 3. Instincts gone astray. *A lot of my behaviors that I now consider defects I once thought of as assets. I didn't realize how selfish it was of me to work the way I did. I always thought it was good to put a lot of time in. But the reason I did it was for petty ego gratification. I never would have identified myself as selfish and controlling. I thought I was a pretty easygoing guy. Another defect I didn't see was my inability to commit. I thought, I work hard and I play hard. I never saw the truth, that I didn't really care about spending time with the people I love. It comes down to not seeing how selfish I was.* GREG

Characteristics. A listing of fourteen common traits of sex addicts compiled by the SEXUAL COMPULSIVES ANONYMOUS (SCA) program. Some of the traits include using sex to feel validated and complete, sex being compartmentalized in one's life instead of a healthy element, the inability to distinguish between sex, love, and affection. *When I first heard them read at a meeting it floored me. It was as if someone had written about me and I didn't know about it. It made a deep impression on me—how much I could identify with the rest of the fellowship. I remember coming home and showing them to a friend of mine saying, "Look at this, look at this, this is me."* VINNY

Chase Your Losses. Common term for one part of the gambling compulsion. The gambler is convinced that he can make up for what he's lost with another try. *I had some money stashed away that I used for lost bets. I'd amass more money, and then drain my funds as I payed off my debts. As I lost, I chased my losses with all my available resources. This is very common for compulsive gamblers. I maxed out my credit cards and got more credit cards, I borrowed against my life insurance policy, I borrowed from family members. Wherever I could, I'd get money to* *get hold of my drug—gambling. It even got to the point where I stole from the family business.* JIM N.

Civilian. A person who does not need a 12-Step program. *My ex-husband bailed me out of credit card debt. I was very envious of him because he saved. I also saw that as a weakness. I knew that he had $60,000 saved and I thought, He should spend that. I didn't think he was manly because he wasn't wild enough, and he didn't do things stupidly the way I did.* NICOLE

Clean. Term used to describe an addict who has not used any drug for a substantial time.

Clean and Sober. 1. Movie starring Michael Keaton about a man who fights both his addiction and recovery. The movie is a good dramatization of the insanity of the disease, and is available on videotape. 2. A redundant phrase used to describe an addict who has not used drugs or alcohol. *In my NA groups we don't say clean and sober. We have a strong sentiment against that phrase. We consider alcohol a drug, and give it no distinction just because it's legal. To say you're an alcoholic and an addict is redundant, and politically incorrect in NA.* RON

Cleveland, Ohio. Where the third A.A. group formed in 1939. That same year the *Cleveland Plain Dealer* published an article about A.A. Requests for help inundated the twenty members of the Cleveland group. Within a few months, the Cleveland group grew from twenty members to five hundred.

Cleveland hosted the first A.A. International Convention in 1950. DR. BOB gave his last talk to the FELLOWSHIP at this convention. His speech stressed the need for A.A. to KEEP IT SIMPLE. The A.A. fellowship adopted The TWELVE TRADITIONS at this convention.

Closed Meeting. 12-Step meetings where attendance is limited to those who are recovering from the particular addiction the program seeks to help. In A.A., closed meetings are for alcoholics only, while in NA, OA, CA, closed meetings are for drug addicts, overeaters, and cocaine addicts, respectively. See MEETINGS.

Closet Drinker. An alcoholic who attempts to hide his drinking by avoiding other people while partaking of favored beverages. *My pattern throughout my drinking was that I would not drink unless I could drink the way I wanted to. I would go to parties and not drink if I didn't want people to know that I was a drinker. Then I would go home and drink all night.* COOPER

Clubhouse. Building or space owned and operated by a nonprofit organization, completely separate from any 12-Step group or organization. Often, grateful recovering people get together and buy a facility, and then rent the place to 12-Step groups. The space provides a place for meetings, social gatherings, and general fellowship. Clubhouses are frequently open for long hours and can provide extra support for recovering people. Some clubhouses have several meetings every day.

Co-Anon. Family groups for relatives and friends of cocaine addicts. Through fellowship and the practice of the 12 Steps, members are better able to cope with life, whether the addict is using or in recovery.

Cocaine Anonymous. A 12-Step program for people addicted to cocaine. The fellowship began in 1982. The program is open to anyone who wants to stop using cocaine and all other mind-altering substances. The steps of CA are adapted from A.A.'s 12 Steps, the only changes being in the First Step, where CA replaces the word "alcohol" with "cocaine and all other mind-altering substances," and in the Twelfth Step, where CA replaces "alcoholic" with "addict."

Codependents Anonymous (CoDA). A 12-Step program started in 1986 in Phoenix, Arizona, by Ken R. and Mary R. The program is a fellowship that seeks to help those struggling with codependency, which can be defined as being addicted to an addict. *What does a codependent say to his mate when he wakes up? Good morning, how am I? Overheard at a CoDA meeting.*

Coffee. 1. By far the most popular drink at 12-Step meetings. Big vats of the stimulating drink get brewed before a meeting and often the pot runs dry. 2. Term used to mean a post-meeting get-together at a local restaurant, as in "You going for coffee tonight?" (You don't have to drink coffee to go for coffee.)

Commitment. 1. The promise and follow-up behavior one makes each day to be free of addiction. 2. To volunteer for, and fulfill, group or individual SERVICE.

Compulsion. The part of addiction that drives a person to start using. It's the irresistible urge to use the drug of choice, despite the destruction and illness that accompany that use. For many recovering addicts, praying to have the compulsion removed or kept away is a daily habit.

Confidentiality. Ideally, what is said at 12-Step meetings, and member to member, is not disclosed to anyone else. This practice encourages people to talk about their problems and feelings, which in turn helps the person to heal. Confidentiality privileges do not extend to 12-Step groups, though. In New York State, Paul C., in an A.A. meeting, talked about a dream he had in which he murdered two people. Turned out that he actually did commit the murders in a blackout. Seven A.A. members who were at the A.A. meeting were forced to testify at Paul C.'s trial. If you have a crime to talk about, it's better to go to a lawyer, clergyman, or psychiatrist, because they have confidentiality privileges.

Conscious Contact. Refers to the working knowledge of the grace of God in one's life. People in 12-Step programs often feel that God directly intervenes in their life, first when they get sober, and forevermore if they work a solid program while practicing prayer and meditation. *The blockage is the issue for me. Conscious contact is about what is there always and my ability to clear away all the blockage so I can hear God. When I'm OK with myself, it clears the channels so God can get through. I'd like to be aware, no matter where I am or what's going on, that the Higher Power is there for me. I try to draw on the spirit to direct my actions.* MARY

I look at it as contact with nature and people, relationships. I thank God every day that he dropped me off right here in the middle of America, not Bosnia or Lebanon. When I see things that are working well in my life, I often say, "Thank you, God." I know he's there for me waiting for me to call on him. MARILYN

Conscious contact occurs if I desire to get in the right place. I must be in a still, quiet place. Breathing techniques help me clear my mind. I pray to my higher power and then put myself in a receiving mode. I try to be conscious of the images that come to me, be they sights, smells. I've had some incredible encounters in meditation. I've found God to be with me. Once in meditation, three beggars came to my door and asked if they could get something to eat. I let them in and I started to prepare some food for them. They said to me, "Tim, kneel down before your God." Of course, telling it just doesn't do it justice. Several times I've felt a presence close to me in the room. I've also smelled a garment that I associate with Jesus. A large part of prayer to me is a matter of my volition or if I'm having a hard time dealing with someone, or if I'm angry at someone, in meditation and prayer I give that to God. I ask for help in dealing with that person. It takes the voltage out of it. I can't do that and still be in a position of arrogance, one-upmanship, power, or whatever kind of game I want to play. I can't do it in the space of quietness and meditation. When I see things in that light, it often helps me to see what I've been doing and I can take care of my part. TIM

I see God's divine intervention for me in recovery. Recently my car broke down when I was on the way to an important business meeting. I was in the middle of nowhere. A fellow came along and drove me to where I was going, turning around and heading back the way he came. Some people might think they were lucky, I think God helped me out. TED

There's the routine. Every morning I get up, get coffee, go back to bed, cross my legs, and pray and meditate. Then I say another prayer at night. It's also the ability to stop and think about things before I make a decision. I remember that I may be in a situation, but that I won't be in it forever. I have a certain set of beliefs about what is the right thing and the wrong thing. On the other side, if I end up doing something I don't like, or I end up yelling at someone, or if I do something that goes against my God-centered life, it doesn't take very long before I start feeling bad about it. In the past, when it was only myself that I worried about, my personal judgment always justified what I was doing. Yet another part is that I'm not afraid to say that I have a conscious contact with God. I don't go out ranting and raving about it. I am surprised at how easy it's been to talk about spiritual matters with my new girlfriend. She says to me, "How do you do this? You seem calm in situations that would drive me nuts, and even if you do get angry you seem to do something that mellows you." I tell her that left to my own devices I get so tied up with anxiety, pain, and anger that I either drink or lash out in some other way. The God-centered life is an alternative to that, and I'm not afraid to admit it. I honestly believe that God is playing a role in my life every day. I used to keep God at an agnostic's arm's length, but I don't think that's possible anymore. GREG

To me, conscious contact means being aware that I am a child of God, and responding to that. COOPER

Control. The power to make changes and direct the course of events. What every recovering person desires when they come into the program, and what they are first told to give up. In place of control, they are told, admit complete defeat, and accept powerlessness. *By nature I am a controlling, rigid person. I like to be in control. Not so much of other people or other things, but I like to be in control of my reactions. I don't like to be caught off guard, and if I am caught off guard I don't want it to show. My drug use was contrary to all that. Consequently, I hit levels that were completely outside my realm of comfort. In the process, I felt like I was running on fumes. Just to get up in the morning (or in the afternoon), dealing with people, going where I had to go, the simple things in life, were just overwhelming. It created a whole process of lying and secrecy and making sure that no one knew what was really going* *on. There was nothing that was just what it was—my life was a game.* MARY

Controlled Drinking. 1. Oxymoron. 2. The many delusive methods used to try to keep the glow, but not get drunk. Including: switching brands, switching drinks, only drinking on weekends (the weekend can start as early as Wednesday afternoon), only drinking after 5 P.M., only drinking after 5 A.M., only drinking beer, only drinking wine, never drinking wine, allowing one drink per hour (only for the most masochistic), alternating one soft drink with every hard drink, taking amphetamines in combination with alcohol, substituting marijuana or downs for alcohol, and so on. For alcoholics, none of it works.

Convention. A mass meeting of board members, delegates, paid service workers, volunteer workers, and general members. Resolutions are heard and voted upon. Specially talented speakers are invited to address topics. Workshops help members address topics of interest. And there's usually a dinner and dance and a whole lot of fun. During the sixtieth anniversary A.A. convention in San Diego in 1995, hotel bars brought in ice cream, frozen yogurt, and extra coffeemakers to entice their reformed clientele.

Counting Days. The practice of announcing the number of days one has abstained from the addiction from which they are recovering. Usually day counting ends at ninety days. *We count our days since we last incurred unsecured debt.* NICOLE

Courage. The moral and mental strength used by recovering people to start the program, and to persevere despite fear, mental and physical cravings, and perceived dangers.

Craving. A strong physical or mental desire to use the drug of choice. Many 12-Steppers pray to have their cravings removed. For some this happens early in recovery. For others, craving never goes away. Spiritual renewal and continued work with other addicts diminish the power of the cravings.

Cross Talk. When one person responds directly to another person in a meeting. Most groups discourage this practice, except in some meetings where the chairperson or leader may respond after the sharing of another.

Cybriety. Playful term used for sobriety by recovering people who communicate with each other over the Internet.

D

Daily Drinker. One who consumes alcohol and/or drugs every day. *I never got through a day without having a drink, and I started out in the morning figuring out when I would be able to drink that day.* COOPER

There were three periods of my life where I drank every day, and they were always when I had left a relationship. The first year and a half of grad school I drank every day. I didn't want to go through the day without drinking. When I had my first job, I realized that I drank every day when I came home. Toward the end of that period I started drinking in the morning too, to get myself going. The last three years of my active alcoholism, I drank every day. For the last year I drank in the morning sometimes, almost always at lunch, and every single night. GREG

Dance of Death. 1. A romantic relationship between two active addicts. 2. The marriage of two active addicts.

Debtors Anonymous. A 12-Step program that seeks to help compulsive debtors. The program began in New York City in 1975. DA groups help individuals through spiritual renewal, which helps them discontinue compulsive debt, and a practical program, which teaches them how to pay off all outstanding debts and develop a spending plan.

Delegate. Individual elected by the area assembly to represent the assembly, and its districts and groups, to the General Service Board of A.A.

Delusion. A false yet persistent belief about oneself, others, or the world. Active addicts often live deluded lives, particularly around their addictions. They go to extreme lengths to deny their problem and live in a fantasy world. 12-Step programs, through the First Step and subsequent steps, help free addicts from their delusions.

Denial. The self-deception that keeps addicts and codependents from admitting the truth to themselves and others. *I took the nonuse of heroin to mean that I am not an addict.*

RON

With Ted, I allowed many years of kiss-and-make-up, always with the promise that it would never happen again. That's why I stayed—I always believed it would not happen again.

Even in recovery I can find myself in denial. In 1987 our daughter Amy, who was in an abusive relationship, arrived at our door covered with blood. She'd had a fight with her live-in boyfriend, John. We took her to the hospital and then to the county attorney's office. Amy lived with us for three months under one rule—that she could not see John. One morning I heard her and Ted talking. She'd been out all night with John, and Ted told her to get her things and move out. Of course she moved back with John. I was so sick that morning that I had to go to the hospital. The first question the doctor asked me was if I had any stress in my life. I said no! Ted said, "What do you mean, you don't have any stress in your life?" I was an emotional wreck, angry at Ted for throwing Amy out. MARILYN

During my active gambling addiction, I had little glimpses of the fact that I was in trouble, but I pushed them aside because I was enjoying too much what I was doing or I thought that I would win and the large sums I gained would make my past sins palatable. I'd strive to accumulate cash and the ends justified the means. JIM N.

Depression. A general state of sadness, inactivity, and inability to think or concentrate. Some believe it is anger turned inward. One of the best home cures for depression is activity. BILL W., who suffered many years of depression, would walk and count breaths for extended periods to help himself overcome it. Many recovering people follow Bill W.'s example and find that regular exercise helps them avoid, or get out of, bouts of depression.

Detachment; also, Detach with Love. To stop interfering in the life of another, because you want the best for that person and now know that everyone must find their own way in life. In the 12-Step culture, it means to turn other people over to the care and protection of God. When you detach, you stop suffering from the actions of other people. *I complained to a neighbor, who happened to be in A.A., about Ted's drinking. He knew I was in Al-Anon and asked me if I wanted my life to be the way it was then forever. I said no. "Then," he said, "you had better detach. Let go and let him drink. He has a right to drink himself to death if he so chooses, and you have a right to a better life. I think it's time you start living it." I immediately turned it over to God when I got off the phone that night. I asked for help and for help to follow through with it. On Monday when Ted was sober, I told him what I had* *done. That I loved him but that I wasn't going to go down with him. I told him, "Things are going to start changing here and I'm going to start living my own life." I sat him down and told him what my guidelines were: dinner is at six, if you are there fine, if not, we eat without you and I'm not going to fix dinner again. When customers called for him or to find out where their supplies were, I'd suggest they call him at the Embers, the Greenwood Lounge, or at the Alpine. He said, "You wouldn't dare." I said, "Try me." I told him that when there were school functions, we'd like him there, but if he couldn't make it that was OK, we'd go without him.* MARILYN

One morning, I was really hung over and sick. Marilyn put the business phone and the house phone next to my bed and woke me up saying, "Honey, I want to tell you something. I love you, but from here on in I'm going to do my own thing." She had turned me over to God. I didn't know it until I read page 120 in the Big Book. She gave me full license to come and go as I pleased, to drink all I wanted. Looking back, I see I went downhill in a hurry. Three months later, on May 16, 1975, I called my next-door neighbor and told him I needed help too. TED

Detox (Short for Detoxification). 1. Process of eliminating drugs from the body, usually accompanied by physical and mental discomfort. 2. Facility used to care for and house persons in the process of detoxification. The usual stay in detox is forty-eight hours, but can last several more days, depending on the individual. *I stayed on a special floor of the rehab. I had a room and a roommate, and there was a smoking room on the floor. I was in detox for about forty-eight hours total, and I spent most of the time in the smoking room talking to others. There was a bunch of people in* *there shaking. It was a place to dry out, away from the general population.* GREG

Disease. A condition in a living thing that impairs its ability to function. The American Medical Association classifies both alcoholism and drug addiction as diseases. According to the DSM-IV, the diagnostic manual of the American Psychiatric Association, the disease of addiction has three major classes of symptoms: 1. Compulsion: loss of control; the inability to control how much you take and being unable to stop; spending too much time using or recovering from using. 2. Tolerance: constantly needing more to get the same high; withdrawal reactions and using the drug to keep them at bay. 3. Impairment: using the drug although it screws up your life, makes you physically ill, and makes you a social outcast; preoccupation with the drug to the exclusion of all else. In general, 12-Step programs view addiction as a disease for which there is no man-made cure. The only hope is spiritual renewal. The 12 Steps are a way to find that renewal.

District Committee. In the A.A. service structure, the District Committee is composed of all the General Service Representatives from the groups in that district. The committee is the conduit between the groups and the Area Assemblies.

Divine Dissatisfaction. How FATHER EDWARD DOWLING, SJ described Bill W.'s motivation and lifestyle. Bill asked him, "Will there ever be any relief?" "Never. Never any!" replied Dowling. Dowling told Bill that his constant reaching for unattainable goals would be how Bill would attain God's goals.

Dr. Bob (1879–1950). He, along with BILL W., founded ALCOHOLICS ANONYMOUS. The date of Dr. Bob's last drink, JUNE 10, 1935, is the founding date of A.A. Dr. Bob's is a legacy of SERVICE. While Bill W. was writing the BIG BOOK and speaking to outside associations to find support, Dr. Bob recruited alcoholics into the program and helped sober them up. According to Bill W., Dr. Bob medically treated and spiritually infused five thousand sufferers. Dr. Bob believed that one's job in A.A. was to "get sober and stay sober and never to be so complacent that we're not willing to extend that help to our less fortunate brothers." He simplified the program to two actions, LOVE and SERVICE. Dr. Bob died of cancer at City Hospital in Akron on November 16, 1950.

Don't Drink and Go to Meetings. The A.A. program is next to impossible to explain, so veterans offer this slogan as a suggestion to newcomers who want all the answers right away, the idea being that newcomers will find the answers they seek if they follow the suggestion. The slogan also acknowledges that every person has to find their own way. *Early on, to every question that I asked, my sponsor would say, "Don't drink and go to meetings." "What am I going to do about my job?" "Don't drink and go to meetings." "What am I ever going to do about my kids?" "Don't drink and go to meetings."* COOPER

Do the Drill. Slogan that reflects the idea that it's best to practice the program and use the TOOLS OF RECOVERY despite how you feel, and whether or not you think it will do any good. *Every morning, without fail, I get up early to pray and meditate because once my day starts it's too late, and I won't remember to do it later. After the phone rings the first time, or after I walk out of the house, it's too late because by then I'm into the day. I've heard people who say that if they are running late, they can say a quick prayer and ask God to help them not drink and do the right thing today. I can't do that because one of my char-*

acter defects is doing things on the fly, and then using the fact that I was in a hurry as an excuse if things don't turn out right. I have to be very deliberate about prayer and meditation. I get up and grab some coffee and pineapple and pray and meditate before I do anything else. I have had occasions where I have to go back and start the day again. I tell myself, no, I'm not leaving the house until I focus myself on spirituality and recovery. I have to fully ground myself in that. Being lazy about it, for me, takes the form of just doing the drill. I feel like, I got to get through this and I'm watching the clock and just moving right through it. I have to force myself to stop and breathe deeply and remind myself that what I'm trying to do is get in touch with God, so that I keep that link all day long. I can't do that by rushing, I can't rush God. God will be with me no matter what, but I have to establish my link to God. If I do rush through, my attitude toward others, God, and myself suffers. I don't think there's any difference in how God views me, but there's a big difference in how I view God. COOPER

Double Winner. A person in recovery for both addiction and codependency. For example, a person who practices the program within the fellowships of both A.A. and Al-Anon.

Father Edward Dowling, SJ. Jesuit priest who heard BILL W.'s Fifth Step. He helped start A.A. in St. Louis. He was a spiritual adviser to A.A. and a great promoter of the movement to the outside world. Dowling explained to Bill W. the condition of DIVINE DISSATISFACTION. As if by divine intervention, Ed Dowling appeared at the door of the old Twenty-fourth Street clubhouse one night when Bill was in a deep depression. Though the two men had never met, that night they talked of God, faith, and gratitude, Dowling often quoting Bill's writings in the Big Book. Bill said the visit lifted him from a terrible dry drunk.

A Drug Is a Drug. Many people, when they first come in, think that if they want to stop using pills it's OK to drink booze; or if they drank, it's OK to smoke a little pot now and then. NOT! 12-Step programs discourage all mood-altering substances because switching addictions happens fast, and you can't have a spiritual awakening if you're all blitzed out on something (at least not the right kind).

Drug of Choice. The favored substance of an addict. Term acknowledges the view that an addict is an addict and the only difference between a coke fiend and a pill popper, or a heroin user and an alcoholic, is the drug used to get high.

Drunkalog (also Drugalog). A long story, told at a meeting, that concentrates on the days of the speaker's active addiction, rather than on recovery. Some people love to hear these stories, but it's safe to say most find them boring. Most prefer stories about how recovery started, how the person practices the program, and how the person has changed.

Drunk (or Drug) Dream. Many recovering people, even after years of sobriety, will have dreams in which they use. Sometimes the dream will be so vivid that the person will wake up and be fearful for a few moments that the dream was real. Another common dream takes the form not of being high, but of knowing that you did get high and trying to plan a way to keep it a secret from your group.

Dry Drunk. 1. A person who behaves as if drinking, but who is physically sober. 2. The period of time in which a person, though sober, behaves or feels as if they're drinking (as in "I've been on a dry drunk for two weeks").

Dual Addiction. Being addicted to more than one substance and/or behavior, usually referring to drugs and alcohol.

Can be any combination of addictions, and can mean more than two. *I was a garbage head. If you told me that gnawing on wood would get me high, the next day you'd see a coffee table with rounded corners and teeth marks. Anything. I had my favorites, but if I had a choice between feeling like I did or feeling different, I'd take different.* *MARY*

Dual Diagnosis. A medical term that means a person has both a chemical dependency and a psychiatric disorder, such as manic depression or schizophrenia. Many people in this situation can be helped with their addiction through 12-Step programs, provided that their psychiatric problems are also properly treated.

DWI. Short for Driving While Intoxicated. The fear of jail time for this crime brings many alcoholics to A.A., but not all. *I had three DWI's before I was twenty-three. After the last one I had to go to an interview to see if the court thought I needed treatment. I talked them out of it. I told them I was a grad student and that I'd had a bad night. Privately I knew I was in trouble and that I couldn't stop, but I didn't want to stop.* *GREG*

Dysfunctional Family. The role of the family is to support, protect, love, nurture, and educate each of its members. Addiction (among many other reasons) often prevents the family from fulfilling these functions. 12-Step programs help families to get on the right track.

E

Earthling. A person who is neither an active addict nor a recovering addict. *I had a friend who also smoked pot, but he had a different view of it. He'd say why don't we roll a pin joint and drive around, get mellow and then get home* *by ten so we can sleep and get up and feel good tomorrow. I liked the concept. I'd say OK, that makes sense. He was much better with this than the rest of us. He'd leave the bag at home. We'd smoke that little joint and my appetite would just be whetted. Maybe I'd be satisfied for twenty-five seconds. His experience of getting mellowed out became my experience of getting more and more frustrated.* RON

Easy Does It. A popular slogan in the program. Addicts and codependents often want everything now, and with impatience and mental anguish will try to get what they want, often with frustrating results. This slogan helps recovering people to remember to slow down and enjoy the process of life. *We don't struggle. We take it easy. The Big Book says that we may have difficulty deciding which course to take, but we don't struggle. I remember that God is in charge and not me, that the world does not stand or fall on my making the right decision. I don't have to worry so much, I just have to go where God takes me.* COOPER

Ebby T. BILL W.'S SPONSOR. Ebby was a member of the OXFORD GROUPS, and he paid a call to the then drunk Bill W. to try to get him to reform. The meeting between the two men made an impression on Bill and he says it led to his spiritual awakening, which led to the founding of A.A. Ebby T. struggled with sobriety for most of his life, but was able to stay sober for his last five or six years. The story of Ebby's and Bill's meeting is found on pages 8 through 12 of the BIG BOOK.

EGO. Acronym for Ease God Out.

Eleventh Step Prayer. The famous prayer of St. Francis of Assisi, and a prayer suggested to those in search of a conscious contact with God. The prayer is part of the study of the Eleventh Step in the book TWELVE STEPS AND TWELVE TRADITIONS. It reads:

Lord, make me a channel of thy peace
That where there is hatred, I may bring love
That where there is wrong, I may bring forgiveness
That where there is discord, I may bring harmony
That where there is error, I may bring truth
That where there is doubt, I may bring faith
That where there is despair, I may bring hope
That where there are shadows, I may bring light
That where there is sadness, I may bring joy
Lord, grant that I may seek rather to comfort
  than to be comforted
To understand, than to be understood
To love than to be loved
For it is by self-forgetting that one finds
It is by forgiving that one is forgiven.
It is by dying that one awakens to Eternal Life. Amen

Emotional Bottom. A recovering person may be straight, but the newness of feeling angry, fearful, hurt, or lonely can become overwhelming. This can be a turning point. The addict may decide to return to the disease, or practice the steps of recovery with a new vigilance. To treat emotional bottoms, the recoveree practices the program in all aspects of their life, not just their addiction. *I was two and a half years sober in the program and a year past my Fifth Step before I felt I understood Steps Six and Seven. They came to me when I reached an emotional bottom. I was running around the Midwest trying to make things happen the way I wanted them to happen, and practicing all the character defects that I had perfected as an active alcoholic—control, manipulation, dishonesty with others—so that I could* *get what I wanted, deciding in my own head what I needed, and deceiving myself. I was practicing all those things to the point where my family was just as concerned about me as they had been when I was drinking. Then I got to that emotional bottom, and I realized that I was just running on empty again. There was nothing in the spiritual bank. Only then did I realize the cleansing power of Steps Six and Seven. Being ready and then humbly asking God to remove our shortcomings. Until that moment, I felt that I had to hold on to the defects and to use them and be powerless over them. When the urge came over me to control, manipulate, or lie, I had to do it. When I hit the emotional bottom, I realized I didn't have to do that anymore.* COOPER

Emotions Anonymous. A 12-Step fellowship of men and women who help each other detach from the problems of anger, anxiety, grief, shame, and self-hatred. The program started in 1971, and now has about sixteen hundred groups worldwide.

Enabling. Behavior that allows an addict to continue the self-deception and self-destruction of substance abuse. Examples: a wife who calls in "sick" for a hungover husband; a father who ignores blatant signs that his teenage daughter is caught up in drugs. Less likely today is Ted's remembrance of a drunken trip to Omaha. *I had a 1963 Buick Electra, and I wanted to see how fast I could get it to go. The first policeman who stopped me clocked me at 95 miles per hour; the second stopped me for a broken headlight; and the third stopped me for running a red light. I was in the bag, but all three let me go.* TED

Enmeshment. To be caught up or tangled in the life of another person, especially within the family. Enmeshed people let the feelings and actions of others dictate their feelings and actions. *If Ted was angry or depressed, I felt responsible. I always thought that maybe if I didn't do something it would all be different. I tried to be more perfect. I tried to be a better wife and a better mother. I tried not to complain when he drank and in general not to rock the boat. I played the martyr role. I didn't ask for anything or to go anywhere. I tried not to make any demands on him as a father or husband. But I felt very sorry for myself. When I think about it today, how sick I was, I just want to puke. How could I have gotten myself like that?* *MARILYN*

Escape. A distraction or relief from something undesirable. Many addicts start with the innocent desire for relief, but end up being ruled by their drug of choice. *At first I thought I gambled because I liked the action. I liked people coming to me for information, and I liked being in the spotlight. As I see it today, when I concentrated on gambling, I didn't need to worry about family, business, or anything else I needed to face. Instead of confronting issues I escaped into gambling.* *JIM N.*

Exactly Where God Wants Me to Be. Common saying that reflects the faith that even though times get tough, God shows the path through and teaches something along the way. Many recovering people believe that the experience of addiction and recovery do have a purpose in God's grand scheme, and they have to participate in painful change for growth to occur. It's another way to say "no pain, no gain."

Expectations. That strange set of beliefs and thoughts about what will happen that never seem to come true. For better or worse, outcomes practically never match expectations. So, for the sake of their serenity, 12-Steppers try to avoid expectations. *Expectations are premeditated resentments. Overheard at a 12-Step meeting.*

Expect Nothing, Appreciate Everything. A suggestion, used mostly in Al-Anon, to those with high expectations of others, the point being that no one can satisfy all your needs, so if someone does something good for you, appreciation is the appropriate response. *I saw my parents and I perceived that they fulfilled each other's needs. I expected the same in my relationship with Ted. When you throw alcoholism into the mix, that expectation can't be met. Today I know that no one can fulfill all my needs, and that I have to fulfill my own. Not to say that I don't have expectations. I expect to go get rocks this afternoon and put them around my bushes. The nice thing today is that if Ted doesn't want to go get rocks, I can go get them myself. I don't have to sit around feeling sorry for myself with the "poor me's."* MARILYN

Experience, Strength, and Hope. What recovering people share in meetings and with each other. This sharing helps to solve common problems, and helps others to find recovery.

F

Faith. For 12-Steppers, it's the belief and trust that a power greater than themselves can keep them straight and help them to lead a sane, full life. For many, faith manifests as an inner security, knowing that no matter what happens, the person can make it through, with God's help. The higher power can be God, the group, the program as a whole, or anything the individual chooses.

FAITH. Acronym for Fear Ain't In This House.

Faith Without Works Is Dead. BILL W. often quoted this line from the Epistle of James. 12-Step programs teach that the only way to keep sobriety and newfound faith is to give it away by helping others. *When I came into the program, I stayed dry for only about three months. I prayed every day, I said I had faith, I read the books, I talked about God in meetings and how he was changing my life. But I didn't do shit. I didn't have any involvement in A.A., and I relapsed. When I finally put a year together, I looked back and saw that I had done a lot of stuff: I chaired four different meetings from the time I had six months, I made coffee, cleaned up after meetings, brought cake to anniversary meetings, and I got involved in Bridging the Gap, a local organization that helps people make the transition between a rehab and joining an A.A. group. This time I stayed sober. I also realize that I don't have to just be of service in A.A. I can do it every minute of the day, at work, at home, in a grocery store—no matter what I'm doing. I can always treat people the way that I know keeps me sober. I can be a prick in a grocery line, or I can laugh off a mistake. I can work with people or I can antagonize them. When I work with a sponsee, I feel like I have the insurance policy of working with another drunk.* GREG

Fake It Till You Make It. Suggestion often made to NEWCOMERS who feel they can't get the program and will go back to old behavior. The suggestion implies that if the newcomer acts according to the steps and teachings of the program, then the program will begin to work and the anxiety will fall away.

Families Anonymous. A 12-Step fellowship of men and women who help each other to recover from the effects of having a child or other close person who suffers from drug, alcohol, or behavioral problems. There are approximately five hundred groups worldwide.

Family Disease. 1. Alcoholism and drug addiction tend to run in families. Substance abuse by parents often leads to substance abuse by children, grandchildren, etc. 2. The substance abuse by just one member of a family affects the entire family, mentally, emotionally, spiritually, and often physically. *On February 24, 1975, I came home drunk. Marilyn says I was standing at the back door with my pants rolled up under my arm. It was then that she realized how sick I was. She went to see our next-door neighbor Walt, who was one of my early sponsors. Walt said to her, "Marilyn, you've never asked yourself this question. Ted may never sober up—do you want to spend the rest of your life living this way?" All of a sudden, nine years of going to Al-Anon came into focus for Marilyn. She was a sick person too.* TED

Family of Origin. The family an individual is born into. Some 12-Steppers feel that their addictive personalities developed as a way to escape the pain and anxiety of their early home life.

Family Visit Kit. Must-have's when you visit your family of origin: Big Book, meditation book, speaker tapes, local meeting list, forgiveness, sense of humor.

Fear. TWELVE STEPS AND TWELVE TRADITIONS says that fear is "the termites that ceaselessly devour the foundations of whatever sort of life we try to build." And this: "The chief activator of our defects has been self-centered fear—primarily fear that we would lose something we already possessed or would fail to get something we demanded." *When I first started going to meetings, I'd wear headphones and listen to my Walkman. I'd keep the headphones on until the meeting started and then put them back on as soon as the meeting ended. I'd run right out after the meetings. I was so terrified of people. For a while, others read me as being intimidating and mean, maybe I was, but I was really afraid. Afraid that I'd find out that* *there was really something horrible about me that would make people want to burn me and spread my ashes in a ditch.* MARY

FEAR. Acronym for Fuck Everything And Run, or Face Everything And Recover.

Feelings. Addicts live in a world of denial when using—denial that there is a problem, and denial that anger, fear, pain, and distrust serve as the addict's motivation and foundation. In recovery, addicts are gently persuaded to talk about how they feel. Talking helps the addict acknowledge the feelings, and it helps them recognize that they can function even if they experience these feelings. 12-Step recovery teaches that feelings aren't facts. *If you asked me what I thought about something, I'd talk for hours. If you asked me how I felt about something, I became dumbfounded and stumbled over my words.* MARY

Fellowship. 12-Step group members share a common experience, a common interest in keeping straight, common feelings, and a common plan of action. They also share camaraderie, and love for each other and a higher power. *At every meeting I go to, at some point, be it early or late, I get an overwhelming sense that everything is going to be all right. I am in the hands of a loving, provident God who is in the people in the room.* COOPER

FIDS. Acronym for Fear of Impending Doom Syndrome. It's suffered by many, even those with years of recovery. Over time most learn to recognize it and laugh about it.

Fifth Step. Action step where a recovering person admits to themselves, to God, and to another person all they know about themselves. For many, taking the Fifth Step means sitting down with a sponsor, or other suitable person, and admitting all faults. A good sponsor will help the person to balance the bad with the good that is in the addict. *I* *skated through the first few months pretty easily, until it came time to do my Fourth Step. I really went through hell over the Fourth and Fifth Steps. There were things where I thought, No way am I going to tell. No one in the world will be able to accept this and accept me. The Fourth and Fifth Steps were my keys to freedom. In a way I feel it was my test of God, and he passed.*

The only way I can complete something is to make an appointment. If I have to have something ready, I will. But a half hour before I'm going to meet my sponsor, Ginny, I'm still working on it, putting in a few things I tried to avoid. I ended up leaving the pages behind when I met Ginny. I had to remember it all and look her in the eye as I told her, because I had no paper to read from. MARY

I did it with my sponsor in my apartment. I lived alone at the time so we had privacy. My sponsor set me at ease. He came over at nine in the morning with a couple of doughnuts, wearing a baseball cap turned backward, joking with me, saying, "Go on, go on, tell me the whole deal." He knew it all already in one form or another, but I sat there and I read it. I read it like a geometry lesson, step by step by step. I had it written out exactly the way the Big Book tells you to do it—columns saying whom I resented, what the cause was, how it affected me, and what part of me was hurt. I filled a whole yellow notepad. My sponsor was used to sponsoring guys who were barely literate, and their Fifth Steps would last forty minutes or so. I was working on three hours, and we were supposed to meet another friend, Scott, to play golf at noon. Scott was outside the door ready to knock when he heard us still working on it. He went back to his car to wait awhile. When it got close to twelve-thirty, he said the hell with it and came knocking on the door. He said, "Anyone who can't do their Fifth Step in three hours is doing therapy." My sponsor sat there and listened to me the whole time. Finally he said to me, "So, do you think you're worse than anyone else?" GREG

FINE. Acronym for Fucked up, Insecure, Neurotic, Emotional.

First High. The start of addiction. *I was a cheerleader and I had a party at my house while my dad was out of town. We rolled in barrels of beer, everyone got sloshed and had a great time, except me. I was hiding in the local cemetery because I had drunk a fifth of vodka and had alcoholic poisoning. My dad found me passed out on a cemetery plot with my two cousins, also passed out. That was the start of my drinking and I was sick for two weeks after that. I didn't think it was the booze that made me sick. I thought it was the cold, damp ground. I also thought that if I didn't drink a whole fifth, or if I just stayed away from vodka, I'd be OK.* AUDREY

My first sexual encounter with a stranger was in a rest room of a department store. I had a sense that I might find something there, and I did. Someone performed oral sex on me. I was stunned by it. I had never experienced that physical sensation. I felt dirty afterward, and felt that I had this incredible secret I had to keep. VINNY

One time, in late junior high, my friend and I stole a bottle of brandy from his grandfather and went way out to this abandoned farmhouse where we used to play all the time. We had the bottle of brandy and we brought one can of coke. We shook the can of coke and then let it fizz out all over the place and we filled the empty part of the can with the brandy. Then we slammed it down as hard as we could. For me there was never a moment of social drink-

ing. We drank it almost straight, with only a half can of coke, as fast as we could. We started walking back to town and I thought this is no big deal. After a little while I started to feel this most wonderful sensation. It was the most beautiful experience I had ever had in my life. It was so fun. I'd fall down in the road and in the ditch, I was all muddy, we were laughing, I couldn't get hurt even if my face hit the ground. I thought: WOW, no wonder! No wonder people do this. RON

Much of my growing up took place in rural Oklahoma, including my first drink. I didn't like the drink at all, it was just a part of the rite of passage. In seventh or eighth grade we drank beer, but we couldn't just go down to the store and buy cold beer. We'd have to steal it first of all, and then hide it down in the basement, or underneath a bed. Beer doesn't stay cold there, so it doesn't have that nice chill on it when you drink it in the cemetery under the dark of night. That was my first drink and it wasn't very exciting to me at all. I drank the beer, but really didn't want any more because I didn't like the taste.

Now, my first real drink was different. At a frat party the host asked me, "What do you want, bourbon and ginger ale?" I told him I wanted scotch. "Water or soda?" He asked. "No, I want scotch. If I'm going to drink I want to taste what I'm drinking. I want to see what it tastes like." I've heard that scotch is an acquired taste. If that's true, I acquired it somewhere between the time I picked up the glass and put it to my mouth that night. I liked it. I've never forgotten the bite of the scotch and then the warm glow that went out from the center of my stomach. I felt a warm, pleasant physical reaction. I liked what it did for me and from that moment on I never wanted the party to stop. COOPER

First Meeting. The start of 12-Step recovery. *I don't remember a lot about my first meeting, but I've been told that I talked for a really long time.* MARY

I'm in NA now, but I went to an A.A. meeting first. It was a big meeting with at least one hundred people there. It was the kind of meeting where four or five people would get up and tell what it was like, what happened, and what it's like now, in fifteen-minute versions. All the others seemed to be relating to the use of alcohol. I cared more about the use of pot. I was a heavy drinker, but it was on again, off again. That meeting did open the door for my recovery. RON

First Step. Here, the addict admits powerlessness and unmanageability in dealing with drugs, addiction, and life. This is the one step that differs among the various programs. In A.A. they admit powerlessness over alcohol; in OA, food; in CA, cocaine; in GA, gambling. NA is the most universal of all programs, they admit powerlessness over addiction. *Here's where the First Step of NA began to mean something different to me—the wording of the First Step. It's why I focus my energy on this program. In A.A. we admit we are powerless over alcohol and that our lives have become unmanageable. If we were to merely adapt that to NA we'd say we were powerless over drugs, or powerless over narcotics. Then we'd be focusing on the same layer of the picture as A.A.—the focus being on the object of the obsession. In NA we say that we are powerless over our addictions. We focus on the underlying condition that causes that obsession. A.A., appropriately, does one thing and one thing well, it deals with recovery from* *alcoholism. The pride and joy of NA is that we have shifted the focus. When people share in A.A. about their obsession, use, and withdrawal, they are focusing on their similarities. In NA, ironically, when we focus on those things, we're focusing on our differences—the things that set us apart. I've sponsored people from one to ten years sober, heroin addicts from the city to other small-town potheads. The focus of our sharing has been our battle with addiction. We get away from the pharmaceutical and physiological aspects of our particular drug of choice. We talk on the feelings level, the self-image layer, and the obsession layer. No matter what the drug is, or who the addict is, there is an amazing similarity among our fellowship in our relationships with the drug of choice.* RON

When I think about the First Step, the thing that stays with me is complete defeat. I didn't get that when I struggled with sobriety. GREG

First Things First. A slogan that suggests recovering people set new priorities and put the most important things before all else. *Sobriety has to be the number-one goal, the number-one priority in my life today. If I'm not sober, then nothing else matters. In the times when I put greater importance on other things—my job, my relationships—nothing works.* COOPER

It's not one of my favorite slogans. It's a little redundant. VINNY

Focusing on Self. 1. 12-Step programs teach that the only thing you can change is yourself, specifically your actions and attitudes. People in recovery make greater progress if they let go of the need to change others and concentrate their efforts on changing themselves. 2. In sharing with others, it is best to stay within personal experience, strength, and hope. Gossip and advice are taboo.

Food Plan. The eating strategy for a member of OA. The recovering compulsive overeater works out the strategy, often with a sponsor, and then abstains from all eating not included on the plan. *You also figure out what your trigger foods are and what they do to you. In your food plan you abstain from these foods. Right now I know from what I've tried to do over the past several years that simple sugars are a trigger for me. I also know that getting too tired or stressed is a real trigger for me. I'm just trying to do the basics, knowing that I can't, God can, so I better let God. I keep it very simple and basic. I plan out what I'm going to eat each day.* TIM

Forgiveness. The process of letting go of hatred, resentments, and anger toward others and self. Practicing Steps Four through Nine, in particular, helps most recovering people through the process of forgiveness. *I know that I harmed myself during the years of living with active drinking and that I have to forgive myself. I've made amends to others I've harmed, mainly my children. I've carried a lot of guilt for a lot of years because of the way I acted. I remember when Pam was in treatment, I remember one of the counselors asking me why I cried so much when we watched the children's movies. We worked on that and I discovered it was the guilt I felt around my own children. The counselor said, "God has forgiven you, why don't you forgive yourself?" I have forgiven myself. I did the best job I could when I had the children. If I'd had Al-Anon sooner, I might have done things better a lot sooner.* MARILYN

I still do carry resentments, but I don't act on them the way that I used to. I don't try to sabotage the people who

hurt me. If someone at work crossed me, I'd go talk to fifteen other people to make sure they all got a certain impression of the offender. I didn't even realize that that was what I was doing. I thought I was just venting, but I was really trying to sabotage that person. When I was drinking, I'd miss my exit driving home on the freeway thinking about how I'd like to beat the shit out of somebody. I don't do that anymore. I haven't beaten anybody up in my head in a long time, but I still struggle with resentments. GREG

For me forgiveness means letting go of resentment and self-righteous anger, realizing that we are all just people and everyone has their good days and their bad days. I can get angry so easily, and I don't have good skills for expressing it. Tonight I was coming in the door and this woman didn't hold the door open for me. Then at the second door, she was opening the door with her key and she looked at me in a way that said, "Oh, do you belong here?" Then we got on the elevator; I felt angry at her but stayed silent. When I got off, she smiled at me and said good night. Here I was running the worst case scenario through my head, ready to yell "fuck you" at her. But she was actually very pleasant. That's the kind of stuff I need to let go of. I feel like the ritualistic practice of the steps will help me with this, rather than just relying on the ideas. VINNY

Forum. The monthly magazine of Al-Anon.

Founders Foundation. An independent group of recovering people who raised the funds and bought Dr. Bob's home. They renovated and furnished the home, and now maintain it for visits by all interested people. The house is located at 855 Ardmore Avenue in Akron, Ohio. Donations can be sent to The Founders Foundation, P.O. Box 449, Akron, Ohio 44309.

Four by Too's. An old expression from A.A. that means Too Busy, Too Tired, Too Lazy, Too Drunk—to attend meetings regularly. Most A.A. groups today rely less on guilt trips.

Freedom. 1. Release from the insanity of active addiction. 2. Liberty to find one's own spiritual path. 3. Result of surrender to the battle against powerlessness. 4. Ability to grow toward the person God wants you to be.

G

Gam-Anon. A fellowship of friends and relatives of compulsive gamblers, who practice the 12 Steps. The program began in 1960 in New York City. Today there are about five hundred groups scattered throughout the world.

Gamblers Anonymous. Fellowship of men and women who help each other recover from compulsive gambling. It began after two men with gambling problems met in 1957. They concluded that to change they'd need to fix certain character defects. They chose to use the principles laid out by Alcoholics Anonymous. The first group meeting took place on September 13, 1957, in Los Angeles, California. Today there are eighteen hundred groups worldwide.

Garbage Head. An addict who will use whatever is available to get high.

General Service Board. In A.A. it consists of seven nonalcoholic friends of the fellowship and fourteen members of A.A. Its responsibilities include safeguarding A.A.'s traditions and service funds. It also oversees the General Service Office, A.A. World Services, Inc., and the A.A. Grapevine, Inc.

General Service Conference. The link between A.A. groups and the GENERAL SERVICE OFFICE and GENERAL SERVICE BOARD. It consists of about 135 members who are Area Delegates, Trustees, Directors, G.S.O. workers, and staff members of the GRAPEVINE. The General Service Conference members meet annually but work year-round. The conference is a forum for sharing and enables each group to reveal their group conscience to the whole fellowship.

General Service Office. For A.A., it is located in New York City. The office employs about ninety-five people, both A.A.'s and non-A.A.'s. The office helps groups with problems, and is a clearinghouse of information for the general public. The office also publishes and distributes over eight million pamphlets and books each year.

General Service Representative. Member elected by a group to represent it in the A.A. service structure, specifically to the Area Assembly.

Geographical Cure. Many addicts, before they find recovery, think that if they can just get away from their family, job, friends, or the town they live in they can stop using and feeling so lousy. So they move from place to place trying to find peace and sobriety. The trouble is that these addicts always bring the real problem—themselves—along wherever they go.

Gift. Many recovering people consider their newfound life to be a bequest from God. *I thought I was raised in a normal home. There was no drinking, but there was dysfunction, and I didn't recognize it until I got into recovery. Had Ted not been alcoholic, and had he not caused problems in the home, I would not have gotten to Al-Anon and been able to get rid of the garbage that I carried in my life.* MARILYN

I've heard it said that recovering addicts are the only people who get a gift and expect a reward. MARY

GIFT. Acronym for God Is Forever There.

God. Word chosen by many in 12-Step programs to identify their higher power. *Early on, whenever I'd hear anyone else talking about God, it was almost enough to send me out of the room. Anyone else's version was really bad and stupid. I had just a fleeting idea of what God was. I didn't know where to begin, I didn't have a religion to fall back on, so I kind of pieced it together. I looked at nature—that trees grew straight up and that rivers flowed to the ocean—and I figured there must be some kind of energy there. My biggest problem was how to apply that to debt. I finally decided that God wants me to take care of myself and I knew I wanted to thrive and be happy. I guess the better part of me wanted to stop owing everyone else.* NICOLE

GOD. Acronym for Good Orderly Direction, also Group of Drunks. Veterans often suggest these two descriptions of God as HIGHER POWERS to agnostic or atheist NEWCOMERS.

God Bless You and Alcoholics Anonymous Forever. Bill W.'s last words to the fellowship of A.A.

God Box. Some recovering people keep a small box to help them communicate with God. They write down what's bugging them and put the paper in their God box. It's a symbolic way to turn a problem over to God.

Going Out. Lingo for relapse, as in "I need to tell you that I've been going out for the past two weeks."

Gossip. Talking about people who aren't present. This practice is highly discouraged among people in 12-Step groups. Everyone needs to feel they can trust one another with honest exchange. To break that trust can result in wariness for a group, or for the program itself. Keeping what is shared in meetings, or person to person, to oneself fosters trust, and willingness to share honestly.

Go to Meetings. A major suggestion of 12-Step recovery. Every person has their own set of beliefs and ideas about their spiritual path. No one can explain fully what the program has done for them or how it works. However, people in recovery know that they have a new life because they've taken the actions of going to meetings, listening, sharing, and learning. No one can give another the answers, but by listening to many people in and out of meetings, and learning about themselves through sharing, 12-Steppers find their way.

Grace. The unearned help from God that allows a person to regenerate. Many 12-Step people believe that grace permits their recovery.

Grapevine. Written by A.A. members, this pocket-size monthly magazine is a journal of facts, motivation, and interpretation of the program. Current circulation stands at about 120,000.

***Grapevine* Meeting.** An A.A. meeting where the topic comes from a reading in the *Grapevine* magazine.

Gratitude. A state of feeling thankful for all the gifts of recovery. Many recovering people try to keep an ATTITUDE OF GRATITUDE no matter what because even the toughest day straight is better than an easy day stoned. *I have gratitude to the fellowship and the program. I try to extend that into my life. On a good day I'm grateful that I have a job that provides money for rent, food, and clothes. When I see homeless people on the street I think there but for the grace of God go I. I'm not always able to tap into that, but I'm usually grateful for the program. I'm not always happy at meetings, sometimes I'm resentful that I have to go to these damn meetings. But when I think about it, I see* *that the program is a wonderful anchor and a beautiful thing to have available. I'm very grateful for that.* VINNY

I often think about what kind of person I'd be today if I hadn't been a compulsive gambler. I'm convinced in my heart and soul that I'm a better person today because of my addiction than I would have been if I had no addiction at all. Before I just went through life helter-skelter, with no goals, no ambitions—except to make money and buy things. Because of my addiction I have gratitude for the things I have today and an appreciation for what it means to be a human being instead of some guy just wandering around this planet. JIM N.

Gratitude List. Many sponsors, when a sponsee is down or feeling crazed, will have the sponsee write down all the things for which the sponsee is thankful. This tool of recovery can change a person's attitude very quickly from glum to grateful.

Gratitude Month. November. During this month, especially around the Thanksgiving holiday, gratitude is the topic for many meetings. It's also fund-raising time for many intergroup offices and central offices.

Greeters. Group members who are assigned to welcome people as they enter the meeting room. For many, the practice sets a friendly tone for the group. Others find being bombarded with smiles, handshakes, and goodwill very uncomfortable and avoid groups that have greeters. About one in twenty-five groups use greeters.

Grief. Suffering caused by loss. Many recovering people, when they stop using, will feel pain over the loss of their old life, despite all the trouble it caused. Many also experience grief for the time they lost while active. Still others experience the pain of losing loved ones for the first time, because they stuffed their feelings while active.

Group Conscience. What the group decides to do, and the ultimate authority of each group. Any decision needed for the group is put to a vote, and the majority rules. The second tradition of A.A. states that God will express himself through the group's conscience. The tradition asserts that the voice of many will lead better than the voice of a few.

Growth. The process of changing for the better. Movement toward strength, tolerance, forgiveness, service, faith, and love constitutes growth. Unfortunately, most growth comes after the pain of change. 12-Steppers believe that a person can never stop growing, because stagnation will lead to greater pain, and even relapse.

Guilt. The feeling of remorse one has for having committed a mistake or offense. Most recovering people feel an inordinate level of guilt. 12-Step programs teach that members are recovering from illness, not from badness, and that feeling guilty is counterproductive. Steps Four through Ten, particularly, help members reduce their guilt.

H

Half Measures. Practicing only parts of the program. In CHAPTER FIVE of the BIG BOOK it states that "half measures avail nothing," and that members must completely give themselves to the program. Partial efforts will not produce partial results, but will produce no result at all. *I feel like I'm in half measures right now. I don't make enough phone calls, or go to enough meetings. I know that my success in the program is tied to how much effort I put into it.* NICOLE

Half Measure Section. The back row at a meeting.

Halfway House. A therapeutic community home in which some addicts live after leaving a treatment center. Living in a halfway house allows the addict to acclimate themselves to society in a slow and gentle manner.

HALT. Acronym to help recovering people remember not to get too Hungry, Angry, Lonely, or Tired. It's also an acronym for Hope, Acceptance, Love, Tolerance.

Higher Power. An existence that can do for a recovering person what he can't do for himself. People in 12-Step programs are free, encouraged even, to define their own higher power. As examples, for some it's the God of their religion, for others the power of the group, and for some it's the natural energy of the universe. Every person has their own way of knowing their higher power. *Before recovery, and even early on in the program, I was scornful of people who professed having faith, or who believed in a power greater than themselves. I took the Second Step progressively because I was so far away from a higher power. First I saw the power as my family—they were the ones who kept me from committing suicide. My family was also the reason I wanted to change. From there I included the people in my group. Not only did I feel a connection with those people, but I also felt a power flowing through them. I knew that there was something greater than us that was working through our lives. From there I went to seeing different signs in my life, and I developed a willingness to look for a spiritual leader in my life. I began to see bread crumbs that showed me that my life was being directed for me. I was being shown the road to take, but I had to make the choices to follow it or not, and I decided to follow it. I now feel fulfilled, whereas I used to feel like a doughnut, empty inside.* JIM N.

Ruth Hock. Secretary to BILL W. during the pioneer days. She typed (and retyped) the original manuscript of the BIG BOOK. Ruth also gets credit for making the serenity prayer a mainstay of 12-Step programs. She received a newspaper clipping with the prayer one day from an anonymous member. Ruth had it printed on cards and began slipping the cards into mailings to members. Now the serenity prayer appears in most 12-Step literature, and is recited at most meetings.

Holidays. As the old joke says, addiction is a threefold disease—Thanksgiving, Christmas, and New Year's. That's why many clubhouses and groups have MARATHON MEETINGS over the holidays. Many recovering people make an effort to stick close to the program during this festive, yet often depressing, time of year.

Some tools used to get through:

- Up your meetings
- Help out at marathon meetings
- Host a party for your recovering friends
- Work with newcomers (there are usually plenty around this time of year)
- BOOKEND your office party, pay your respects, get the hell out if you feel nervous
- Give of yourself
- Embrace the spirit of the holidays

Home Group. The 12-Step group that a recovering person attends most regularly, and feels most dedicated to. Many select their SPONSOR from their home group. *The thing that struck me about my NA group was that the more screwed up you were, the more welcome you were. It was the first place I'd ever been like it. Defects were like military decorations. I thought, This is great, I'm home.* MARY

Honesty. Telling and facing the truth. This is a foundation of recovery. When one admits powerlessness, the need for help, and the exact nature of one's wrongs, restoration begins. Practicing honesty throughout recovery is essential, but it's also a dramatic change for most 12-Steppers. *I expected lies to get me through a situation, help me forget something, or get me out of it. Yeah, I may feel terrible afterward, but it should work for now. Eventually it stopped working.* MARY

Hope. A cherished desire, with the expectation of achievement. *I feel like I've experienced so much darkness in my life that I need to look forward to the light to come. Working with other people in SCA, I see that we are all trudging along this road. I don't know what the outcome will be, but I believe that I'm doing the right thing. I believe in the promises, and that I may not get what I want, but I'll get what I need. The promises do materialize if I work for them. I don't think that I'll ever reach a summit, but I'm hopeful that the general state of unrest in me will change. I know that more will be revealed and that I'll be taken care of.* VINNY

Hostage. A person involuntarily controlled by another. It's said that active addicts and codependents don't have relationships, they take hostages. *I got married early on in my Navy career. My wife and I met while I was in college. When I was in the Navy and she was a sophomore in college, we got married. She was the first full-time hostage that I ever took. I've taken lots of hostages, but with her I realized as we got married that I had a hostage on my hands. I thought, What am I going to do now?* COOPER

HOW. Acronym for three foundations of recovery: Honesty, Open-mindedness, and Willingness.

How Do You Spell Relief? Slogan of 12-Steppers who believe that all addicts and codependents are basically the same—only the drug or method for escaping oneself differs. Once in the program, people spell relief H-I-G-H-E-R P-O-W-E-R.

How Important Is It? Slogan to help recovering people remember that they can get tied up in knots over insignificant events and personalities. The wise person recites the serenity prayer when troubled, seeks the counsel of other recovering people, and then decides if the situation is worth trying to change.

How It Works. The title of CHAPTER FIVE of the BIG BOOK. Also the vernacular for the first eight paragraphs of the chapter, which include the 12 Steps. This shortened version of the chapter is read at the beginning of many, if not most, A.A. meetings. *How it works, you ask—slowly and well.* COOPER

Humility. The ability to see the true relationships between oneself, other people, the universe, and one's higher power. *One of the gifts of recovery is being able to connect with more people—both in and out of the program. When someone new comes into the program and is practically drooling on themselves and can't complete a sentence, I can look past that to see the person and their pain—and myself. Then I can also use that ability with people outside the program, and get past the me versus them thing.* MARY

When recovery took hold, I didn't have any of the luxuries I once loved. But I had something I'd never had, and that's humility. It allowed me to forget that I didn't have anything. AUDREY

It took a great deal of humility for me to go to the gambling treatment center, and another good dose for me to go to GA. The first GA meeting I went to was held in a

church, and I hadn't been to a church in at least eight years. I didn't know where the meeting was in the church, and it was a hell of a scary experience for me. I found out that there were other people like me and that I wasn't alone. I wondered what kind of people would be there and I found out that they came from all walks of life. There were people who lived in their vans, and others who had been very well off. Gambling had brought us all to the same starting point. JIM N.

I

I Am Responsible. Slogan used as the theme for the 1965 Thirtieth Anniversary International Convention of A.A. The message is that if a suffering alcoholic reaches out for help, A.A. members want A.A. to be there. For that, each member is responsible.

I Can't, God Can, I Think I'll Let God. Steps One through Three, abridged.

If Ya Wonders, Then Ya Is. Saying that acknowledges that people who wonder if they are addicts probably are. Nonaddicts don't think they might be addicts.

If You Want What We Have, Do What We Do. Often said to NEWCOMERS who don't trust that change is possible. They're gently told that the way to a new life is to follow the SUGGESTIONS of the program, and emulate those who know the way.

Insanity. Among 12-Steppers, it's defined as doing the same thing over and over and expecting different results. *I feel I was functionally insane. I'll never know "what if?" I was able to accomplish things, but I still had great difficulty in areas of my life, particularly intimate relationships. I also had trouble dealing with anger and anxiety. I repeated the* *same thing over and over again, expecting a different result.* VINNY

I knew on that final day that I had three choices—to go on to insanity by drinking; to go on to insanity and probably suicide through not drinking; or to give A.A., God, and the steps a try. I had to be that desperate, that defeated, because I'd been able to not drink and I went nuts dry. GREG

Intergroup. An office, supported by local groups, that acts as a clearinghouse for information. They answer phone calls of people in need of help, or from people who need general information. They also sell literature and help coordinate group activities.

Intervention. A group of concerned persons get together and plan a meeting with an addict. They then confront the addict and tell her how her addictive behavior affects them, and how they see the addiction hurting her. The goal is to break through the addict's denial system and to get her to enter a treatment program. It is beneficial to have the guidance of a professional before attempting an intervention.

Intimacy. 1. Revealing one's true nature. 2. A warm friendship that develops out of long association. 12-Step programs encourage both definitions. In Steps Five and Nine, defects, strengths, and wrongs are admitted to others. The fellowships also encourage individuals to discuss themselves in meetings and among one another. This strips away the barriers of isolation that aggravate the disease.

Inventory. The Fourth Step calls for a searching and fearless moral inventory, and the Tenth Step suggests a continuous personal inventory. The Fourth Step inventory is usually done on paper. The idea is to look at oneself honestly seeking both the good and the bad. In Steps Five through

Nine, one takes actions to have the bad removed and the good enhanced.

ISM. Acronym for I, Self, Me; Incredibly Short Memory; or I Sabotage Myself.

Isolation. The act of avoiding others. Active addicts avoid others by practicing their addiction. In recovery, fear, anger, and resentments can cause people to avoid others and stay alone. It's a bad habit that needs to be avoided. Once you join a 12-Step program, you never have to be alone again unless you want to be. See SOLITUDE. *Ironically, I always wanted to be in control. The only way I could exercise any control was to isolate. Increasingly, it became less about what others thought or about creating an impression, and more about hiding and doing what I needed to get high. I'd do anything so I would not have to sit in my own skin. I was too filled with drugs, self-obsession, and self-loathing to keep any friends. I feared an internal explosion. What if I'm with you and it all comes out? We might both find out what a horrible person I really am.* *MARY*

Issues. The endless myriad of feelings, defects, circumstances, resentments, personalities, and internal struggles that 12-Steppers face and work through in recovery. *Issues are like tissues; remove one and another follows. Overheard at a 12-Step meeting.*

It's the First Drink. Most alcoholics wish they could take one or two drinks and then leave it alone, but once an alcoholic puts booze in the body, a physical craving takes control and the person is powerless to stop. Avoid the first drink and the cycle does not begin. A.A. and other programs advise to avoid the first one, and you don't have to worry about how many you take. *The train's caboose* *doesn't kill you, the engine does. Overheard at a 12-Step meeting.*

J

William James, 1842–1910. An American psychologist and philosopher. His book *Varieties of Religious Experience* inspired Bill W.'s early work with alcoholics, and many of the philosophies of the program. One quote from the book, "Religious experience is a fundamentally private affair between the individual and God, as the individual conceives God," sums up the 12-Step philosophy respecting a higher power. Bill W. described James as a "spiritual founder of Alcoholics Anonymous."

James Club. An early suggestion for the name of the program that became Alcoholics Anonymous. Much of the wisdom of the program at the time came from the Epistle of James in the New Testament.

The John Larroquette Show. An NBC comedy series in which John Larroquette plays the role of John Hemingway, an alcoholic recovering in A.A. Attendance at Tuesday night meetings went down the first season of the show, when Hemingway struggled with his newfound sobriety. David Crosby played his sponsor, who eventually went back out. Lately the show centers around Hemingway's love life, and Tuesday's meetings get good crowds again.

Judging. The act of placing another above or below oneself. The program teaches that all are equal, with strengths and weaknesses, and for personal serenity it is best to see others in that way. It's also suggested that recoverees try to identify rather than compare.

June 10, 1935. The date of DR. BOB's last drink, and the founding date of ALCOHOLICS ANONYMOUS.

Carl Jung, 1875–1961. Swiss psychiatrist whose work with Rowland H. inspired two key elements of the 12-Step recovery program. He told Rowland that he was hopeless, unless he could achieve a vital spiritual experience. Rowland sought such an experience and joined the Oxford Movement. He met Ebby T. and helped him get on his feet. Ebby T. then sought to help Bill W. Ebby imparted the knowledge of hopelessness and the need for a spiritual change that laid the foundation for Bill W.'s spiritual experience, which led to the founding of Alcoholics Anonymous.

Just for Today. Slogan. Recoverees don't make long-term promises about abstinence or living right. They do it one day at a time and leave tomorrow to tomorrow. *Just for today, I won't use, and I'll try to live in accordance with my higher power. Overheard at a 12-Step meeting.*

K

Keep Coming Back. 1. No one gets fixed in a 12-Step program. Newcomers and veterans find that the program works best when they go to meetings regularly. This slogan encourages 12-Steppers to continue to use the program to get better. 2. Chant recited at the close of many 12-Step meetings. Variations: Keep coming back, it works. Keep coming back, it works if you work it. Keep coming back, it works if you work it, so work it. Keep coming back, it works if you work it, so work it, you're worth it. 3. Often said to people in a bad or crazy spot (sometimes sarcastically), after they share at a meeting.

Keep It Green. Many 12-Steppers with long-term recovery like to keep in close contact with newcomers, visit rehabs or detoxes, and hear other's stories because it keeps the memory of the horrors of active addiction fresh (or "green") in their minds.

Keep It Simple. Addicts tend to intellectualize and complicate everything they do. This slogan reminds recovering people that the program is very simple, and it works best if practiced that way. The slogan also encourages recoverees to cherish and lead a simple life. *One of my favorite slogans, and something I like to remind newcomers of. It's a great reminder to me to not get overanxious, frantic, to try not to overdo. So often that's where my problems come from, because we overcomplicate things, or we're not seeing things for what they are. Boiling it down can really help. This is something that carries over to my creative work too—because keeping it simple often results in beauty.* *VINNY*

Kinsman. A clean and sober bikers' club located in northern California. They practice the principles of NA and A.A., and they sponsor and support many clean and sober biker runs. Similar clubs exist throughout the United States.

KISS. Acronym for Keep It Simple, Stupid.

L

Lamplighters. An A.A. group on the World Wide Web that started in 1990 with six members. They lend support and suggestions to each other as they pursue recovery. They also encourage people to attend live, face-to-face meetings. Lamplighters can be contacted by E-mail at lls-approval@world.std.com

Lateness. *The only meeting one is ever late to is the first one. Overheard at a 12-Step meeting.*

Laundry List. A check sheet of the troublesome characteristics shared by adult children of alcoholics. The list is provided to newcomers at ACOA meetings to break down denial and show them that they are not alone anymore. It's a fourteen-point list. Here are some examples:

- We seek approval and lose our identity in the process.
- Angry people and any personal criticism frighten us.
- We either become addicts, marry addicts (or both), or find another compulsive person to fulfill our need for abandonment.

Let It Begin with Me. Slogan. 1. Forcing change in others and in situations is impossible, but over time change from within is possible if one keeps the focus on self. 2. Addiction is passed on from one generation to the next. To stop the legacy, one must change and break the cycle (of course there's no guarantee). 3. 12-Steppers believe that service is a key to recovery. This slogan encourages individuals to take on responsibilities and commitments.

Letting Go. 1. Turning one's life, another person, a thing, or a situation over to a higher power. 2. Accepting unchangeable circumstances. 3. Allowing others to make mistakes, and to have successes, without interference. 4. The process of becoming at peace with something you don't necessarily like. The following essay describes what letting go means:

To let go does not mean to stop caring, it means I can't do it for someone else.

To let go is not to cut myself off, it's the realization I can't control another.

To let go is not to enable, but to allow learning from natural consequences.

To let go is to admit powerlessness, which means the outcome is not in my hands.

To let go is not to try to change or blame another,
it's to make the most of myself.
To let go is not to care for, but to care about.
To let go is not to fix, but to be supportive.
To let go is not to judge, but to allow another
to be a human being.
To let go is not to be in the middle arranging all the
outcomes, but to allow others to affect their
own destinies.
To let go is not to be protective, it's to permit another
to face reality.
To let go is not to deny, but to accept.
To let go is not to nag, scold, or argue, but instead to
search out my own shortcomings and correct them.
To let go is not to adjust everything to my desires, but
to take each day as it comes, and cherish myself in it.
To let go is not to regret the past, but to grow and live for
the future.
To let go is to fear less and love more.
—Author Unknown

This was a real brainteaser for me when I first came in. I heard it all the time, but I couldn't comprehend. I thought to myself, How? How do I do that? What does that mean? Finally learning over time how to let go has become such a gift. I don't say I can always do it, but I can do it now better than I ever could. This slogan has helped me with my whole life. At my job I have to deal with many different people. My last directing job I was in charge of twenty different performers and technical people. There are many different personalities, yet there's the super-objective and the job to get done. Trying to get through it while holding on to all the barnacles doesn't work. I've learned to let things go. My problem is that I don't forget things very easily. I might think I've let a problem go, but I really haven't. On a day-to-day, minute-to-minute basis, it works pretty well for me. VINNY

Liberty (magazine). A Fall 1939 article about Alcoholics Anonymous in this national periodical resulted in eight hundred calls for help to the then small New York office.

Life on Life's Terms. Suggested way to live. 12-Step programs encourage members to practice acceptance in daily living, and to take what comes and make the most of it. *I like the saying, "When life gives you lemons, make lemonade." I try to live today, not tomorrow or yesterday. God is in charge of my life, and what he gives me today I'll try to live with. We've started a new business and lots of people have tried to discourage us, but I'm excited about it and believe that it will turn out the way that God wants it to turn out. There's a friend of mine in the program who always says, "Trust God and do what's in front of you."* MARILYN

There's a rebellious part of me that wants to alter the world so that I fit. What I need to do is work my program and incorporate the steps, so that I'm the one who changes. I've heard that recovering people are the only ones who get a gift and expect a reward. My living life on life's terms is the opposite of that. Being clean is a gift, but it doesn't mean I get the reward of the whole world changing to suit me. MARY

My reaction to losing my business would have been completely different when I was still drinking. I would have placed blame on the industry that was doing this to me, and I'd have been paralyzed with resentment. Now I've

accepted the situation and am taking actions that will help me make a living in another way. TED

Listen. A suggested way to learn the program—attend MEETINGS and try to pay attention to the wisdom and experience of those who have more time in the program.

Literature. Most programs try to put the experience, strength, and hope of their members into writing, so others may read and learn about the program and learn how to practice the program. The programs publish books, pamphlets, magazines, cards, and audiotapes, all to carry the message to those who still suffer. Many longtime members read literature regularly to keep the program fresh in their minds. See the Bibliography for a listing of literature for recovering people. *Certain things I've read stand out over others over time. Out of a reading there are usually one or two sentences that strike me at any given time, and they're often not the same ones. I try not to become too academic. It doesn't take much for me to understand on a thinking level. On an application level, the living level, I'm not as quick. When I was in treatment, my psychiatrist said to me, "You know, Mary, no one is too dumb to recover, but some people are too smart." I'm not brilliant or anything, but I can really use the head stuff as a deflector. Literature has been helpful, a sentence here or a paragraph there. The challenge is how do I live what's in the book?* MARY

Live and Let Live. Slogan that suggests that members commit to living their own life, and allowing others to live as they choose. *It says to me to detach with love. Go to the next step and don't let others get you all bent out of shape. People have feelings and don't always act the way I want them to. I know I don't always act the way people want me to. I have good days and bad. I heard another person on a tape say that some mornings he feels blue and wants* *the world to go away. If he stays that way for long, he knows the men in white coats will come to get him. Some mornings he feels happy and ready to take on the world. If he stays like that too long they'll come and get him too. No one's chance at life is very good, and that's how I try to see it.* TED

I can't change any other person. Even though I think I know what's best for them, I have to let them go on and do what they have to do, while I go on with my life. A few years ago I participated in an intervention on a friend who is obese and extremely controlling. We were trying to help her, but when I saw her reaction I knew that nothing we could do would change her. She would go on and be that controlling, obese person, and she is. Now when I see her I think of her as a child of God and remember that God loves her just the way she is. It's up to God to make the changes in her life. I need to keep the obsession of another person out of my mind. MARILYN

Live for Today. Suggested way of life. It means to turn out worry about the future, and remorse about the past, and to do what you can for your new way of life today. Also stated as Live in the Moment, Living in the Day, Stay in Today. *Once you get on a debt repayment plan, you can start to live for today. You no longer have to worry about how you're going to fix your life, or hope against hope that you win the lottery. Your needs are cared for and you can be happy, today.* NICOLE

For me today, the present, is what matters. The past I have no control over, it is done. The future I don't necessarily have any control over. But today, in my actions, I have control over how I will respond to things and how I react

to situations. I am the person I am today because of all that I have done in the past. This puts more importance on today because tomorrow's person will be based in part on today. If I can live within my morals and boundaries today, I'll be a better person today—and tomorrow. JIM N.

Living Cyber. An online A.A. group that takes its name from a play on words of the title of the A.A. booklet *Living Sober.*

Living Sober. A great book filled with suggestions on how to avoid the first drink. It is a collection written by A.A. members for new A.A. members.

Lois W. The cofounder of Al-Anon and Alateen, and Bill W.'s wife. Her story is featured in the book *How Al-Anon Works* and her autobiography, *Lois Remembers.* Lois was an ambassador for both A.A. and Al-Anon. She attended every international convention from 1950 to 1988 (when she died). She also traveled the world visiting groups, even in such far-off places as Kenya, New Zealand, and Hong Kong. Lois is one of the most loved and admired people in the 12-Step culture.

Long-term Recovery. A relative term, depending on the beholder. A person with three days thinks someone with a year has been straight forever, while someone with four years thinks the same person is a pup. Most would agree that ten years or more justifies the term.

Lord's Prayer. The prayer said at the close of most 12-Step meetings. The prayer, attributed to Jesus Christ, says:

Our Father, who art in heaven, hallowed be thy name.
Thy Kingdom come, thy will be done
On earth, as it is in heaven.
Give us this day our daily bread

And forgive us our trespasses
As we forgive those who trespass against us.
And lead us not into temptation
But deliver us from evil
For thine is the kingdom and the power and the glory
Forever and ever, Amen.

The prayer encompasses many of the principles of the program, including following God's will, forgiveness, and the desire to avoid temptation. Some feel that because it is a Christian prayer, it should not be recited in a program that claims it has no affiliation with any sect or denomination. Most think it's a good prayer and don't care that Christianity is the source.

Losers Group. Unorthodox group of Alcoholics Anonymous that meets at the Peninsula Alano Club in San Mateo, California, on Wednesday nights at eleven forty-five. The group encourages those who can't sleep, don't have a job, don't have a real job, don't have a life, or don't have anywhere else to go to stick with them. If you're sick of rules like stick with the winners, no cross talk, early to bed, early to rise, meetings should begin and end on time, don't throw food, one share per person, or no cigars, then the losers group may be for you.

The Lost Weekend (novel and movie). A true-to-life story about an alcoholic man in New York City who gives up a weekend in the country so that he can stay home and drink. Both the novel and the movie do a fabulous job depicting the horrors of the DT's. Highly recommended.

Love. The true explanation of How It Works. *I can even love my body today, even all this fat around my belly. After all, it did what I asked it to do—protect me from my feelings.* *TIM*

M

Major Changes. Many sponsors will recommend that a sponsee not make any major changes in the first year of recovery. Major changes include quitting a job, ending a relationship, starting a relationship, moving, buying expensive items. Recoverees feel restless, irritable, and discontent in the first year or so. These major changes might seem like an answer to the discomfort. By not making major changes, the recoveree benefits in two ways. First by learning to ride out uncomfortable feelings. Second, by not taking actions that might be regretted after the thrill is gone.

Manipulation. The act of using tricky, controlling, or insidious techniques to get what one wants. While manipulation is used by many active addicts and codependents, recoverees try to abstain from it and instead rely on honestly asking for what they want and letting go of the results. *My husband started coming home. For the longest time he never came home and now he was home all the time. He started finding bottles and pillboxes, and he confronted me saying I was an alcoholic and drug addict. I said, "How dare you say that about me?" I told him it was all his fault because he was never home and that I drank and took drugs because he never was there to help me. I brought up the death of our baby and he started to feel bad. This manipulation allowed me to keep using without a hassle, for a while.* AUDREY

Marathon Meetings. Some groups and clubhouses hold meetings every hour, or every other hour, at special times such as Thanksgiving, Christmas, and New Year's. A marathon meeting can also be one constant meeting for a day or two.

Marty M. The first woman to get sober in A.A. She founded the National Council on Alcoholism and led the battle for the acceptance of alcoholism as a disease. She also wrote the book *The Primer on Alcoholism.*

Martyr. A person who goes beyond all reason in serving others, in order to feel better about themselves. Martyrdom is also often used as a form of MANIPULATION by active addicts and codependents.

Mayflower Hotel. In AKRON, OHIO. The site where BILL W. made the crucial decision to try to contact another alcoholic. This action led to his meeting DR. BOB. The two then went on to found ALCOHOLICS ANONYMOUS.

Meditation. 1. The process of quiet reflection or contemplation. 2. A written piece meant to guide others in reflection.

For me prayer is talking to God and meditation is listening to God. I have to admit that I don't read my meditation books as often as I should. I talk a lot to God—when I'm working around the house, when I'm in the car, times when there's no one else around. I must hear him, because there are times when I get answers and think that must have been God. He often tells me there's more than one way to skin a cat. MARILYN

Meditation is the other side of the coin. If I put out my stuff to God in prayer, I need to let God put out his stuff to me in meditation. MARY

The process for me can vary. Sometimes it's very formal, sometimes it's in a group, sometimes it's just for a minute, sometimes it's for thirty minutes. I've learned to yearn for it, but I also tend to resist it. If I take the discipline and do it, within seconds I'm grateful that I did. Meditation is like going to a meeting for me. There's a contact that reminds me that I'm on a spiritual course in life that I don't under-

stand, but that God understands. I try to just let go and be quiet and see if I can listen for something. Or I try not to think. I use a mantra as I learned in TM several years ago. Not so much because I believe in the Buddhist forces that may or may not be there, but because the mantra is a meaningless word, so I'm not thinking. It's a mindless exercise and I can allow other things to happen. When I have abstinence I get a clear mind and I can hear that voice of God or the universe so much clearer. JIM C.

Meeting Makers Make It. Slogan. Recovering people who attend meetings regularly have an easier time staying clean than those who don't.

Meetings. Regularly scheduled engagements where recovering people gather to share their experience, strength, and hope, to achieve and maintain freedom from obsession and craving. Meetings are a staple of recovery. They have an inexplicable ability to renew the strength and resolve of members. Meetings remind you who you are and that recovery must come first in your life. The sharing of others has the power to renew hope.

Types of Meetings:

Anniversary. A celebratory meeting in honor of a member's additional year of recovery. Also can be a celebration of the group's additional year of existence.

Beginner. Meetings that focus on helping newcomers learn the program.

Big Book. Parts of the book *Alcoholics Anonymous* are read and discussed.

Business. Special meetings, often held directly before or after the regular meeting, in which group conscience, elections, or financial matters are discussed and put to a vote.

Closed. Meetings open only to those seeking recovery from the addiction that program was created to treat.

Discussion. The meeting leader will pick a topic, or ask others to suggest a topic, and then the group shares on that topic. Most groups welcome members to share whatever they want to, even if it does not relate to the suggested topic.

Exchange. Where members of another group come and speak.

Literature. The topic is picked from a pamphlet or book published by the program or another source. The reading becomes the discussion topic.

Open. Any meeting that welcomes all people, whether they are recovering from the program's particular addiction or not.

Outside Speaker. Where a nonaddict with some expertise will speak to the group. (Very rare today.)

Panel. Often used at beginner meetings. Two or three experienced recoverees will lead the meeting and respond to the sharing of group members.

Speaker. 1. One person will tell their story for twenty minutes or so, and then the group members share. 2. One, two, or three people tell their story, and no other sharing takes place.

Step. Where the topic is one or more of the 12 Steps.

Topic. The group leader, or another member, will start the discussion by choosing a topic for the meeting. *I think meetings are very important. When I leave a meeting, I'm much less anxious than when I went in. When you go to a meeting and share about something that's been causing you pain, the people across from you are nodding in understanding agreement. Before the meeting, you might think you're the only one who deals with such problems. I* *remember, just a few weeks back, I thought everything was going along smoothly, but in the car on the way to a meeting, Ted snapped at me about something. My mind said, What's that all about, what did I do? I realized that I didn't do anything. At the meeting I shared my feelings of anxiety, panic, and bewilderment. I like things when they're good, I guess we all do. When they're out of order or out of kilter I don't like it, I feel uncomfortable. I shared all about this and everyone's head nodded up and down, as if to say, "We've all been there." This particular church has an A.A. meeting and an Al-Anon meeting on Friday nights. Many couples go together and split off to the different meetings, then a group of friends goes out to eat after the meetings. On this night my friend Jackie asked if I wanted to ride to the restaurant with her. I said no, I'd go with Ted. We got in the car and as we drove an old comedy act was on the radio. Ted started to laugh and he reached over and took my hand in his. Whatever animosity we felt toward one another when we got to the meeting was gone after the meeting.* MARILYN

The pressure is off after I go to a meeting. I feel much more at ease and comfortable in my own skin when I'm at a meeting and I come away from it feeling the same way. When I got out of treatment my counselor insisted that I read the Big Book every day and go to a lot of meetings. TED

I get many things from meetings. Listening to other people's stories helps me to rediscover the things inside me that I forget I have. It helps me remember where I once was, and what I'm grateful for today. Meetings recharge my batteries and revitalize me. They also help me to talk about things I need to get out. I can get any chaos that's inside me out. Talking to others allows me to hear of their experiences in similar situations, and this gives me strength to carry on. JIM N.

Men's Groups. 12-Step groups that serve the special needs and concerns of men. Many men use these groups to address issues that they do not feel comfortable discussing in the presence of women. These groups often foster a level of intimacy and fellowship that men cannot achieve in mixed groups.

Merchandise. All kinds of items are marketed toward people in recovery. Some of the items include bumper stickers (the best being "Insured by Smith and Wilson"), books, pamphlets, anniversary medallions, medallion holders, posters, angel pins, audiotapes, meditation tapes, magazines, key chains, address and phone books, refrigerator magnets, greeting cards, plaques, teddy bears, book covers, bookmarks, baseball caps, T-shirts, sweatshirts.

Misery. A state of sustained unhappiness or distress. Once recovery begins, pain is inevitable, but misery is optional.

Misery Parade. Drunks walking around the block in the morning waiting for a bar or liquor store to open. One gift of sobriety is never having to join the parade again.

Mr. X. A code name for BILL W. used by his psychiatrist, Dr. Henry Tiebout, when he quoted Bill in his papers. Bill sought Tiebout's help for depression in the summer of 1944. In speeches, Tiebout often spoke of his A.A. patients and how their spiritual awakenings through the program opened them up to therapy, their emotions, and to life itself.

MMM. The Three M's. Newcomers to A.A. and NA learn that they can best work the program with these three tools—Meetings, Meditation, and because it's suggested to avoid new relationships in the first year, Masturbation.

Monopoly. Bill W. stated very clearly what 12-Step programs still profess today—12-Step programs have no monopoly on recovery, and have no monopoly on God. 12-Step programs provide a simple set of tools that help many to find a higher power and recovery, but both can be found in other ways too.

Moral Inventory. The Fourth Step suggests recoverees "make a searching and fearless moral inventory of themselves." Most sponsors will ask that this be done in writing. Inventory takers write down all they can remember about harm they've done to others and to themselves, and the reasons why they've done this harm. Many sponsors suggest that the negative be balanced by the positive and ask recoverees to write down their good points too. The Big Book contains a simple form for taking a moral inventory. It suggests making three columns. In the first column you write down the names of people you resent; in the second column you write the reason you resent each person; and in the third column you write what segment(s) of you is affected by each person. After many years of workbooks and supposedly more effective methods, the Big Book's simple approach to a moral inventory is popular again.

More Will Be Revealed. Slogan of ACCEPTANCE often said to struggling newcomers. As recovery progresses, it becomes apparent that the journey will never be complete. More and more defects, strengths, desires, fears, and feelings appear to the conscious mind, and this will be so until the end.

Murphy Brown. Television show about a hard-nosed reporter who is also a recovering alcoholic. While Murphy's addiction and recovery played a big part in her character early in the show's existence, they have become a nonissue in recent years.

My Best Thinking Got Me Here. Slogan conceding that the wisdom of the program is a much better guide to life for recovering people than their own thoughts and desires. Left to their own devices, addicts will use again.

My Name Is Bill W. A pretty good biographical television movie about the life of A.A.'s cofounder. The movie often airs on cable television stations.

N

Nar-Anon. A 12-Step program for family and friends of drug addicts. The program began in 1967 in California, and now has groups worldwide.

Narcotics Anonymous. A 12-Step program of complete abstinence from all drugs. The program began in California in 1953, and now has over twenty thousand groups worldwide. Following A.A. and Al-Anon, NA is the third largest 12-Step program. It is the most open of all the 12-Step programs for addicts. Meaning NA doesn't care what drug a person is addicted to—heroin, pot, pills, other narcotics, or alcohol. They see addiction, not the substance, as the problem, and they try to help all addicts to find a power greater than themselves that will keep them away from the first use. *When you compare NA to A.A., you see that the structure has differences, but the people in both are striving for the same thing.* MARY

The NA Way. The monthly international journal of NARCOTICS ANONYMOUS. The digest invites all members to submit articles, and the opinions expressed in each article reflect those of the person who wrote it. It's a great tool for recovery because it gives a fresh set of literature to subscribers each month. It also keeps readers up to date on upcoming NA events and conventions.

Never Alone. A slogan that tells members they never again have to go through any struggle, or joy, by themselves. *At my first meeting, in April 1966, what struck me was "my God, I'm not alone." Thirty other women sat in the room and all of them had the same problem as me. Before that, I was sure that I was the only person in town who had this problem in my home.* MARILYN

Newcomer. A relative term. To a person with thirty days, a person with a week is a newcomer; while to a thirty-year veteran, someone with seven years is a newcomer. Most would classify someone with under two years CLEAN as a newcomer, unless of course that particular program has been around less than two years. The newcomer is the most important person at a meeting because recovering people need to help others to help themselves. Newcomers keep this vital process alive. *To newcomers we basically say, Keep Coming Back. I heard someone share in a qualification that to newcomers it may seem like people are not very warm, that everyone knows everyone else, or that people aren't reaching out to you. I think this is very often the case. But, as the speaker said, it's because this is a place for you to discover whether you belong here, and we don't want to push anyone. We are dealing with sex and intimacy issues—and major boundary issues. We don't always know what someone's reaction is going to be if you say hello or give them a hug. Mostly I try to encourage people to give it a few meetings. I try not to talk too much to newcomers. I try to say welcome and introduce myself. I do give my number, even knowing that nine times out of ten they won't use it. Just to make them feel welcome, and that they are not alone. I've seen so many people come and go over the years. It's wonderful to see someone come in* *and work the program, experience the great changes and embrace the 12 Steps.* VINNY

New Group. Two essential ingredients for the formation of a new group—a resentment and a coffeepot.

New Relationships. Newcomers learn to avoid new relationships in the first year. A new love can become all a person thinks about, but recovery needs to be the focus in the beginning. Sponsors have also seen breakups send the recovering person back to active addiction.

New York, New York. Where A.A. group number two formed. Now it's the site of the A.A. General Service Office and A.A. World Services, Inc. Al-Anon, Gamblers Anonymous, Gam-Anon, and Sexual Compulsives Anonymous also headquarter in New York City.

90-in-90. Many of the programs, especially those dealing with addicts, recommend that newcomers go to ninety meetings in the first ninety days. This helps to quickly acclimate the person to the program, and gives the individual a sense of accomplishment very early on. The intense meeting schedule also helps the addict develop a sense of hope, despite the struggles of the first three months.

Ninth Step. Where a recovering person makes direct amends to the people he's harmed, provided that doing so will not injure anyone. *Step Nine would have been hard on me if I had done it the way I wanted to do it. I would have immediately gotten on an airplane and flown to all different parts of the country to tell people that I'm here to right this terrible wrong that I did to you. The fact is that God just kept putting people in front of me.*

My family was just so glad that I wasn't drinking and that I was in A.A. that I heard from them that my recovery is my amends to them—and I believe them.

I had moved away from a city before I got sober, and I'd

been away for six years. I thought I'd never have to see many of the people I'd harmed, but God had other plans and he moved me back and put me right back in the same associations where I'd met with those people. I found myself averting my eyes when I'd see them at church or other places. I couldn't go on doing that, so I began making amends. It wasn't hard once I started doing it.

There were other people who were dead and gone. I remembered hearing a man tell that he had lost his five-year-old daughter in a car accident. He didn't cause the accident, but he was drinking at that time and he doesn't even remember her funeral. He said that he made amends to her through God. I did the same thing with some people.

The first occasion I had to make amends did not go the way I wanted it to go. My sponsor had to remind me that I was doing it for me, not for the other person. I went into it expecting forgiveness. But that's not the purpose of the Ninth Step—the purpose is to clean up our side of the street. COOPER

Nonsmoking Meetings. The days when the people in the last row could not see the speaker because of all the cigarette smoke are over. Most public buildings, including churches, forbid smoking. Unfortunately, most clubhouses have not caught up with the times and still allow smoking. This drives people away. Many recovering people, now that they have a choice, will not attend meetings where smoking is allowed. There are still enough meetings for smokers who can't recover from their nicotine addiction.

Normie. A person who is not addicted to anything.

NUTS. Acronym for Not Using The Steps.

NYPD Blue. Television program in which a main character, Detective Sipowitz, is an alcoholic struggling to recover in

A.A. He fights the program pretty hard. Many recovering people are rooting for Sipowitz to find a higher power.

O

Obedience to the Unenforceable. 12-Step programs have no rules. Instead the groups and service structure operate under the 12 Traditions, which are guidelines for the survival of the programs. No one can be forced to adhere to the traditions. However, they work, and people in 12-Step programs know that the survival of their group and the program as a whole is necessary for their own survival. Most recoverees try to conform, if not for the good of all, then at least for their own good.

Obsession. An enduring preoccupation with an unreasonable thought, idea, or feeling. For ADDICTS and codependents, a common obsession centers on believing that they can continue the same behavior and not have the same troubling consequences. *My husband became violent, and I'd get a beating when I got home because he'd want to know where I was. I could take the beatings. One time, though, while he beat me one of my Baggies opened and spilled pills all over the floor. He called his family to come over and see what was going on. There I lay beaten on the floor, still trying to save my pills. I cried and tried to hide my pills from all of them. I was able to save some of them. I ended up in the emergency room that time with thirteen holes in my head from a high heel shoe, and a broken arm. But I still had some of my pills.* AUDREY

A day in the life of a compulsive gambler:

Sunday morning I'd get up early with a knot in my stomach because there were late games on Saturday and I

didn't know the score. This could make a big difference on how much money I had to bet with that day. I also might have to make up on Sunday what I lost Saturday night. Monday was the last day of the betting cycle before you pay your bookie on Tuesday. I'd get up and muster the guts to look at the scores. I'd either celebrate or be pissed off.

After that, I'd immediately look at the day's games—who's playing whom, read the columns and the injury reports, watch ESPN and hear predictions on the point spreads. The bookie would be open from ten-thirty to noon. I'd need to formulate my bets—how much I would parlay, would I bet the over and under, if I did would I take the minus or plus? By this time I had a couple of gallons of acid churning in my stomach, and several knots too.

I'd finally get my bets down on paper and call the bookie. The line would be busy and I'd feel frustrated. I'd wait a minute and hit redial, still busy. It's getting closer to noon and I know that he's going to be closing soon and I need to get my bets down. Finally I get him and lay down my bets.

Now it's game time. I'd usually watch on TV, but if the game happened to be on the radio I'd listen with headphones and cut the lawn or work in the garden in an attempt to work off some of the adrenaline pumping through my veins. I'd go in at halftime and check the scores, feeling happy or sad. I'd beat myself up if a game wasn't going my way—telling myself what a fool I was for betting the way I did. At the same time I'd start worrying about the late afternoon games and whom I'd bet. The bookie would be open between two-thirty and three and I had to start figuring out my wins and losses so I could see how much I'd be able to bet, or how much I needed to make back, in the later games. I'd plan out whom I would bet on, what games I'd parlay. I always seemed to get the bets down just in the nick of time. If I didn't go outside and work, I'd watch two or three games at a time flipping back and forth. I'd flip to the sports ticker on CNN if the scores weren't reported fast enough on the game channels.

After the end of the games, I'd tally my wins and losses. Then I'd break for dinner with my family, trying to show that I was a part of the family. Then I'd start worrying about the Sunday night game. I'd call in and place a bet, always without my family knowing about it. I'd use the phone downstairs or sometimes drive to a pay phone—whatever it took. I'd stay up and watch the game. If I had a good day, I'd watch the sports report on ESPN and feel excited by the plays that led up to my wins.

If I lost, I'd be up worrying about where I'd get the money to pay off my debt. I'd also begin planning for the Monday night game. I'd lie awake worrying about the lies I told my wife. I'd obsess about my indiscretions at work too. JIM N.

Old-timer. A person with many years in the program. It's all relative, but most will agree that someone with over twenty years is an old-timer. *How to become an oldtimer in A.A.: Don't Drink and Don't Die. Overheard at a 12-Step meeting.*

The Old Twenty-Fourth. A.A.'s first clubhouse, located on Twenty-fourth Street in New York City. It was famous for its long corridor that led to the meeting room in back. Many saw the corridor as symbolic of their long trudge to recovery.

Once an Alcoholic, Always an Alcoholic (Also True for Addicts). Slogan to inform recovering people that no matter how long they're clean, they can never go back and use their DRUG OF CHOICE like a *NORMIE*.

One Day at a Time. The most popular of all the program slogans. The only day a recovering person has to deal with is today. Tomorrow will be the day to deal with tomorrow, and yesterday is over and done with. Addicts tend to see not using forever as impossible, so the program breaks recovery into a manageable chunk—don't use today. It's a very effective philosophy for those who practice it. *I have to let go and turn my will and my life over to the care of God every day. I ask God for his will and the courage to carry it out. I try to take a daily inventory of my actions and correct what needs correction. It's a lot easier now for me to admit when I'm wrong and keep my mouth shut when I'm right (I love that part of the program).* MARILYN

One Is Too Many, and One Thousand Is Never Enough. The active addict's predicament. Once started, stopping is impossible.

Only You Can Make the Decision to Be Sober. Slogan that tells people that their recovery is up to them. The fellowship and a higher power can only help and support a compliant participant.

Open Mind. Many addicts come to recovery with a belief system that seems fixed. The program advises that newcomers be open to new ideas about spirituality and how to live life. Change will be necessary, but can only happen if the addict is open to it. *Keeping an open mind is not something I do quickly. I tend to be judgmental and impulsive. I'm a snap decision maker. The second thought might be, Keep an open mind.* COOPER

Overeaters Anonymous. 12-Step program for people seeking to recover from compulsive overeating. The program began in 1960 in Los Angeles, as the result of a meeting between three people who sought to help each other with their eating problems. At first the program took a more psychological approach to members' food problems, not seeing overeating as an addiction. That model soon changed, and OA patterned their program after that of Alcoholics Anonymous. It remains that way today. This worldwide program now has over ten thousand groups. Because the addicts in this program struggle with food, complete abstinence is impossible. Abstinence from compulsive overeating is possible, though. The program recommends that members develop a sane relationship with food, and then use the spiritual tools of the program to help them maintain that relationship.

Oxford Groups. The fountainhead of Alcoholics Anonymous. The movement, founded in the early 1920s, sought to enrich members' spirituality through a rigorous practice of early Christian principles. Their six main principles were:

1. Surrender to a God of your understanding.
2. Examination of one's conscience.
3. Confession of character defects to another.
4. Practice of making amends when someone has been injured.
5. Meditation and prayer.
6. Quiet time, following meditation and prayer.

When EBBY T. made his call to BILL W., he was a member of the Oxford Groups. When Bill W. needed to find a drunk to talk to that weekend in Akron, he was helped by an Akron clergyman and HENRIETTA SEIBERLING, who were also members of the Oxford Groups. DR. BOB, along with his wife, was also a member when he met Bill W. Bill and LOIS W. joined shortly thereafter.

What became A.A. grew up out of the Oxford Groups. Much of the spiritual philosophy of A.A. came out of the Oxford Groups. In addition to the six principles listed above, the Oxford Groups operated under six basic assumptions:

1. Men are sinners.
2. Men can be changed.
3. Confession is a prerequisite of change.
4. The changed soul has direct access to God.
5. The age of miracles has returned.
6. Those who have changed must change others.

DR. SAMUEL SHOEMAKER, Bill W.'s spiritual mentor, was the leader of the Oxford Groups in America.

Bill and Dr. Bob succeeded in bringing many other alcoholics into the Oxford movement. Over time, though, the drunks and the mainstream members began to split. Guilt and rebellion resulted from the Oxford Groups' demands for absolute moral rectitude. The alcoholics feared that these feelings could end up getting them drunk. They also did not like the four absolutes of the Oxford movement: absolute honesty, absolute usefulness, absolute purity, and absolute love. In the Big Book, Bill W. wrote: "We claim spiritual *progress,* rather than spiritual *perfection.*"

Another issue that separated the alcoholics and the Oxfords was that the Oxfords wanted publicity, while the alcoholics wanted anonymity. After learning much about what to do, and what not to do, Bill W. and his fellows split off from the Oxford Groups to start their own groups, which later were called Alcoholics Anonymous.

P

Page 70. In the first editions of the BIG BOOK, CHAPTER FIVE began on page 70. Members then lovingly referred to the popular reading as "Page 70," rather than "HOW IT WORKS."

Page 449. An often-referred to page in the BIG BOOK, which discusses acceptance. The writer of this story, "Doctor, Alcoholic, Addict," basically says that just as he could not recover until he accepted his alcoholism, he cannot be happy unless he accepts everything as being just as it's supposed to be at that moment. When recovering people feel troubled by people, places, and things outside their control, friends and sponsors often advise them to read page 449.

Pain. The mental, emotional, and sometimes physical discomfort that comes during the growth process. Active addicts avoid pain and growth by using. Recovering people try to accept pain, and use the spiritual tools of the program to work through it. Popular sayings in the program: no pain, no gain; pain is inevitable, misery is optional. *When I was active, and my girlfriend would tell me how much I hurt her, I'd tell her if she thought it was hard living with me, imagine how bad it is to live as me.* *RON*

A Part Of. Many addicts, before they find recovery, do not feel as if they belong in their families, communities, or in the world. Many nearly destroy themselves using drugs to change their feelings, so they can fit in. 12-Step programs help these addicts learn that they do have a place and a purpose when they take part in the fellowship and service of the group, and that they don't need to destroy themselves to find peace. *I had never felt rejected, because I'd learned manipulative skills. I was fairly bright and my par-*

ents gave us a lot of cultural advantages that I was able to manipulate. I was always able to get people to do what I wanted them to do. Teachers, friends. That became a real problem for me. I learned how to manipulate people rather than how to deal with them. That was part of feeling alien. It was the only way I knew to get what I wanted. Other people worked for what they got, I learned very early on that I could con my way to what I wanted. That left a lot of time for me to do other things I wanted to do. But I always sensed that there was something missing, and that even though people had rules, they were comfortable with that. They belonged. I always felt that they knew something that they weren't telling me. But when I drank, I didn't feel that way. I could join in, and not feel alien. COOPER

Pass It On. 1. When a recovering person thanked BILL W. for his help, Bill would commonly say, "Pass it on." 2. The title of a book about Bill W. and how the A.A. message reached the world, published by A.A. World Services, Inc.

Patience. The quality of sustained tolerance under stress. It's a quality many must learn for the first time in recovery.

Patient. The attribute many feel BILL W. forgot to include in the description of alcoholism in HOW IT WORKS. "Remember that we deal with alcohol, cunning, baffling, powerful, *and patient!*"

People Pleaser. One who overserves and/or tries to be the center of attention to get approval from others. These people tend to judge themselves based on what others say about them. *I learned how to mother early on. My mom worked in the fields beside my father so I was left in charge of my two brothers and my sister. I learned very early how to please my parents and I was always striving to do things right and have all the jobs I was given accomplished when* *they got home. I needed approval very early on. I got a lot of strokes for having everything right. I think that started the intricate part of my life as a people pleaser.* MARILYN

Perfectionist. 1. One who tries to be entirely without fault or defect. 2. One who expects others to be entirely without fault or defect. 3. One who expects his environment to be without fault or defect. 4. One who expects his work to be without fault or defect. 5. One who expects others' work to be without fault or defect. 6. One who expects the products of his environment to be without fault or defect. 7. One who goes on and on in an attempt to perfectly cover all perspectives.

Periodic. An ADDICT who does not use every day, but who goes on sustained binges regularly.

Phone. A tool of recovery that's often referred to as the way to have a meeting between MEETINGS. Recovering people often use the phone to call another person when they feel tempted by their addiction, or if they are experiencing stress. They also use the phone to simply contact others as a way to keep in touch with the new way of life. *When I first came in, I'd often come home after a meeting and spend the rest of the evening talking to other program people. I also made calls during the day. The phone has been an essential tool for me, especially in the beginning.* VINNY

Phone List. 1. A list of recovering addicts and their phone numbers kept by an individual for use when the person needs someone to talk to. 2. A listing of the names and phone numbers of a particular 12-Step group, usually compiled voluntarily by group members. *My date book is filled with the numbers of recovering people. It's been invaluable. I've been given the gift of surviving in spite of myself. From the beginning, I tried to develop a rapport with people that was not hinged on crisis. That way when* *a crisis did occur and I needed to speak to someone, I was much more comfortable. I encourage people to call me too. If I've not talked to you, my chances of calling when I need to are greatly reduced. If I have the opportunity to call someone with a bullshit reason, the call will eventually work its way into the real reason I needed to call. The phone list is part of the process of starting relationships and becoming accountable. It sets up the foundation before the earthquake.* MARY

Pigeon. A lovingly insulting term for a new SPONSEE, or a NEWCOMER.

Pill Addicts Anonymous. 12-Step program for people addicted to prescription medications.

Pink Cloud. The feeling of elation that often comes in early recovery. The body is detoxed, the mind is beginning to work, and a sense of hope enters the addict for the first time. There's a sense that everything is going to be all right—often for the first time in an addict's life. The pink cloud tends to disappear when the recoveree begins to see that staying clean a day at a time takes hard work. *I heard someone describe himself as being on a pink cloud. He was told "this too shall pass." I don't think pink clouds are bad as long as the foundation of recovery is there. They will pop. It's that initial rush when one realizes "I'm free." They are God's gift to struggling people who have not yet experienced the freedom of the 12 Steps. Pink clouds are dangerous when they're not accompanied by the foundation of knowing who we are, what we're about, and what we need to do.* MARY

Pioneering Days. The early days of A.A. before the BIG BOOK, before offices, before pamphlets, when the only means of carrying the message was from one drunk to another.

Pitiful and Incomprehensible Demoralization. A phrase used widely in 12-Step literature (originally in Chapter Three of the BIG BOOK) to describe the consequence of addiction.

Pity Pot. The illusory place an addict sits when he feels sorry for himself, despite having the grace of God in his life.

PMS. Abbreviation for Poor Me Syndrome, or Pour More Scotch.

Poor Me, Poor Me, Pour Me Another Drink. The course and outcome of sitting on the PITY POT too long.

Postcards from the Edge. A novel and movie, written by Carrie Fisher. About a young actress who gets in trouble because of her addictions, and then struggles to stay clean. The novel describes the disease's cravings and insanity with powerful accuracy.

Powerless. Being unable to control yourself, and lacking the ability to change on your own. One can be powerless over addiction, and people, places, and things. Most find a bit of peace when they're able to admit powerlessness. *I believe I'm an addict and I believe my problem is my addiction, not alcohol or pot or pills. None of that stuff forced its way into me. It's my addiction that forces me to keep at it. It's not about a specific drug. In NA I practice the program for all of Mary—the addiction is part of me, not something outside me. I'm not cured as soon as I get the drugs out of my system. When we say we are powerless over our addiction, it's more about us.* MARY

For me admitting powerlessness was like a giant sigh of relief. Today I'm glad to admit that I am not alone, and that I don't have to be alone, and ultimately that I don't have to try to make it alone. VINNY

Right after I came into DA, I got a freelance job that paid me $10,000 in a very short time. I thought I had it made, *so I left the program and spent the money really fast. Then I realized I was right back where I'd always been, in debt and poor. I think it was then that I realized my powerlessness.* NICOLE

Prayer. Talking to GOD in word or thought. It's a positive action that demonstrates a willingness for help. In the story "Freedom from Bondage" in the BIG BOOK, the writer tells the story of reading an article about resentments by a prominent clergyman. The article suggested that if you resent someone, you pray for that person and ask that they get everything you want for yourself. Even if you don't mean it, do it anyway. The article said that if you do it for two weeks, you'll lose the resentment. The alcoholic tried it and it worked. Now it's a tool used by many 12-Steppers. *When I pray for someone instead of for something, it changes me. Prayer also helps me to see things in a mature, loving way, rather than in a childish, selfish way.* TIM

I have come to see prayer as a way to express my gratitude to my higher power for the gifts of my life. I don't pray for good things to happen, or for me to be in a certain place. I do pray to see the bread crumbs in my life, because I believe my life is laid out for me now and that a higher power is directing my life. There's no use in praying for things, because the things I need are going to be provided. JIM N.

Pressure Meeting. A tool used in DEBTORS ANONYMOUS. A member will choose two other members, ideally a man and a woman who have over three months of abstinence, to help the individual construct a spending plan, figure out a debt repayment plan, or find a job. It is each member's responsibility to assemble the pressure group. The other members are there to listen, offer encouragement, and share their EXPERIENCE, STRENGTH, AND HOPE. *I did it after keeping records of my spending for three months. It was a very loving atmosphere. We sat down and said the serenity prayer together. The other two looked at my records and then helped me to develop a spending plan. First we wrote an ideal spending plan, where I wrote down all the money I wished I could spend and all the different ways I could spend it. Then we wrote an actual spending plan, based on the money I truly had. We emphasized making sure I was getting the things I needed, and even some pleasurable things like a movie occasionally or going out for coffee with friends. It's a very personal process, but the pressure group helped me to find a way to take care of my debt, yet still be good to myself.* *NICOLE*

Pride (Short for False Pride). The inability to admit one's faults. One of the SEVEN DEADLY SINS that can destroy a person's recovery. *I didn't share at the meetings because Ted got sober in A.A. for a short time and then went back to drinking. I didn't want anyone to know this. I thought that everyone who went to A.A. immediately stopped drinking. My false pride kept me from sharing that he was drinking.* *MARILYN*

Primary Purpose. The main reason a 12-Step program exists. For example: In A.A., the primary purpose is to stay sober and help other alcoholics achieve sobriety. NA's primary purpose is to carry the message to the addict who still suffers. In Al-Anon the primary purpose is to help the families of alcoholics. Other programs use similar language, substituting the program's chief focus.

Principle. A standard or discipline of conduct. In 12-Step programs the principles are the 12 Steps and 12 Traditions.

Principles Before Personalities. A recovering person can often focus on the negative aspects of others in the group, to the point where it can affect the person's serenity and recovery. The programs advise focusing on the steps and traditions, and letting others be who they are.

Privileged People. Despite the terribly high dues one pays to get into a program, 12-Steppers know GOD as few CIVILIANS ever will.

Progress. To move toward a higher, better, or more well-developed stage of recovery. Addiction is progressive, but so is renewal. *The disease progressed within me through years of unmanageability. Recovery progressed within me despite many setbacks.* VINNY

Progress, Not Perfection. CHAPTER FIVE of the BIG BOOK says that members seek spiritual progress, not spiritual perfection. Many 12-Steppers try to integrate this concept into their daily lives, in matters both spiritual and worldly. It means being able to attempt something and not have to do it one hundred percent correct, and being able to take joy from the effort itself. The phrasing came out of BILL W.'s assumption that the four absolutes of the OXFORD GROUPS would cause rebellion in too many alcoholics and make spiritual recovery impossible for them.

Projection. 1. To determine the outcome of future events or predicaments in one's mind. 2. To take characteristics of self and assign them to others. *When I get upset with someone, I'm often seeing something in that person that I deny in myself. The source of the anger can be helpful to look at to understand me.* JIM C.

Promises. A popular reading from the Big Book. After the description of Step Nine, it says:

> If we are painstaking about this phase of our development, we will be amazed before we are halfway through. We are going to know a new freedom and a new happiness. We will not regret the past nor wish to shut the door on it. We will comprehend the word serenity and we will know peace. No matter how far down the scale we have gone, we will see how our experience can benefit others. That feeling of uselessness and self-pity will disappear. We will lose interest in selfish things and gain interest in our fellows. Self-seeking will slip away. Our whole attitude and outlook upon life will change. Fear of people and economic insecurity will leave us. We will intuitively know how to handle situations which used to baffle us. We will suddenly realize that God is doing for us what we could not do for ourselves.
>
> *Alcoholics Anonymous*, pages 83–84.
> Reprinted by permission.

The program opened up for me. I quit fighting God and the world and my business. As it says in the Twelve and Twelve, I began to desire humility more than anything else. I began to walk in the steps. The Big Book says that what used to be the hunch or the occasional inspiration gradually becomes a working part of the mind; that began to happen for me when I surrendered. For the first time, I feel at home in the world. That's the gift of this program. I'm forever grateful that I don't take alcohol into my body today, but I'm infinitely more grateful that that means I've been given the gifts of knowing what to do and of feeling a part of the world. I'm not perfect, but every morning I can say that I'm at peace with God, the world, and my fellows. COOPER

Q–R

Qualification. A speech made at a meeting by a 12-Stepper that describes the person's active addiction, and their recovery. It's a tongue-in-cheek term because no one has to qualify for a 12-Step program. Anyone who says they're a member is a member.

Rationalization. An excuse that makes sense to the perpetrator, but is clearly in error to others—especially a SPONSOR.

Reaching Out. 1. The act of asking others for help. 2. The act of giving help to others. *My boyfriend broke up with me the night before Valentine's Day and I went on a binge. I called a friend I had once acted out with who was now in the program and he helped me. That's when I got in the program to stay.* VINNY

I'd just been released from jail. My parents were away, so I was in their home alone. I remember praying and praying for help. I remembered a friend of mine who I once used with. I knew he had gotten clean. I tried calling him, but all I got was a busy signal. Finally, with sincerity, I said, "You know, God I'm trying to find help. If you don't let me get through to this person I'm going to walk through the plate glass window and die. It's your call." I'd been trying to call this guy for two hours. The next time I tried, he answered. He had been on the phone with his sponsor for two hours. He took me to my first meeting. I've been clean ever since—ten years. MARY

I'd had enough, so I called our doctor, our lawyer, and our minister. The minister called back and said a member of

our church was also a member of Alcoholics Anonymous, and he'd be happy to talk to me. I said OK. That afternoon Ralph B. called me. He told me he was an alcoholic, but had been sober sixteen years. He said he'd be glad to speak to Ted when he got back to town, and that there was a program for me. He wanted to know if I'd be interested in talking to someone from Al-Anon. I said yes. MARILYN

Real Alcoholic. A phrase used in the BIG BOOK that some people in A.A. use to describe themselves. Are there fake alcoholics?

Reality. 1. The truth. 2. What's actually happening, as opposed to what the mind may think is happening (although they can sometimes be the same).

Record Keeping. A suggestion of the DA program, that members keep a log of all the money they spend. This helps recovering debtors to understand their spending patterns and to write budgets. *In my first meeting I heard about writing down my numbers. I keep a little notebook and write down everything I spend down to the penny. I've been doing it for six years. It's worked well, and you really don't grow out of it.* NICOLE

Recovering. Term used to describe the process of healing from the effects of addiction. People in 12-Step programs say they are recovering, rather than recovered, because they need to keep up the work of the program to stay clean and continue to grow.

Recovery. 1. The time span in which one has worked a 12-Step program and stayed sober. 2. The ceaseless process of healing that takes place when one stops acting out their addiction and picks up the tools of a 12-Step program.

Regular Meetings = Insurance. *A sign spotted at a 12-Step meeting.*

Rehab. A rehabilitation center. A therapeutic environment in which addicts live for several weeks with other addicts, and are immersed in learning about their disease and the tools of recovery. Many, but not all, rehabs use the 12 Steps as a basis for their recovery program.

Relationship. The association between people. Relationships are usually an unmanageable struggle during active addiction, and a somewhat manageable struggle in recovery. 12-Step programs help recoverees accept the shortcomings of others, as they begin to accept their own shortcomings. *Certain things my sponsor John said still reverberate in my mind. One of them is about Step Eight when I put together my list of the people I had harmed, and I was talking to him. I described this guy and that woman and what I had done to them, and he listened. He said, "Tell me about the people you just aggravated the shit out of." I said, "What?" He said, "You know, the people who just don't want to have anything to do with you." What he was getting at was—"OK, you've told me about the people over whom you've held so much power and authority that you could wreak havoc in their lives. Tell me about the people who just don't ever want to see you again." John helped me to humbly see that most of these people would not agree that I had greatly wronged them. They'd say that I did not have that kind of power over them. Mostly, I just aggravated them and they got tired of having to deal with me, and they didn't ever want to see me again.* COOPER

My first meeting was December 9, 1972. I went to the meeting scared to death. There were six people there. I sat through the meeting and it had more impact on me than any one hour of my life. I remember leaving that meeting and I saw a squirrel in a tree and I realized that I hadn't

seen a squirrel in years. I went home and I wrote the only poem that I've ever written in my life. It was about the ability that I felt in my heart to love. Whatever happened in that meeting, it seems like it broke something open. I think it's that influence that has allowed me to not try to control or buy other people, but I could now see others from an emotional level. I don't think that I could ever do that before. Since entering the program I'm a lot less self-centered and selfish. My relationships are much more rewarding today. JIM C.

Today things are easier. I can tell Ted what I feel without fear of being punished, and I'm not afraid of him anymore. I never had to be afraid of him physically, but he could punish me for a week or two by not talking to me. Of course, I did the same thing to him. It's much easier now to share with him how I feel about something. I know full well that I might not get what I want, but at least I can tell him what I want or feel or need. It took a long time in recovery to get to this place. Even when Ted got sober, I feared he would punish me or he'd walk away if I asked for something that was too much for him. I was always afraid that Ted wouldn't want me or need me anymore. As I grew in my own recovery, I saw that Ted's sobriety meant he could live without me—but I also saw that I could go on without him too. The people and the principles of the program would give me all the support I needed to deal with whatever changes came about. We're together today because we choose to be together. MARILYN

We let each other cook in our own grease. TED

Religion. 1. *Religion is for people who want to stay out of hell. Spirituality is for people who've already been there.* 2. *With religion you can hear the word of God. With spiritu-*

ality you see the word of God in practice. Overheard at 12-Step meetings.

Research. A slang term for a relapse. It's said you can go out and use to research whether you are truly an addict. Or you can research whether active addiction has gotten any better.

Resentment. Anger focused on a perceived offense, hurt, or insult. The BIG BOOK says that using is but a symptom, and that in the Fourth Step we must get down to causes and conditions. It also says that resentments are the number-one offender. In the Big Book's guide to a Fourth Step written inventory, it suggests listing in the first column the people for whom you feel resentment. *When active, I went out with this very wealthy guy and I was very resentful that he didn't just give me a lot of his money. I resented the* New York Times *because I wasn't a big* New York Times *writer. I resented Nora Ephron because she's a woman who made it really big. I especially resented co-workers who did well.* NICOLE

Resentments Hurt *Me* Most. *A sign spotted at a 12-Step meeting.*

Retreat. A period of withdrawal (usually over a weekend) where members of a 12-Step program gather for prayer, meditation, and to be immersed in the program's teachings. It's a time to eat, sleep, and live the 12 Steps. *Nowadays if I go on a retreat, I like to stay in a motel. I don't like the bunk beds, the cold showers, and the skinny towels. Early on I didn't give a shit, I was into sobriety. I miss that attitude somewhat. There's a good men's retreat in the fall. It started about eighteen years ago, and I went to the first five or six years. It gets to the point, though, that newcomers look up to you too much. You hear a bunch of*

Fifth Steps and all that. My soul wasn't getting as much out of it as my ego, so I stopped going. JIM C.

I love retreats. There are workshops all day. In the evening after dinner there might be a show with different groups performing their own skits. Often, talented speakers share. There's usually a special spiritual meeting on Sunday morning, where each person talks about a particular subject. Everybody there gets involved in something. Workshops might be on such topics as grieving, sexuality, any one of the steps, or the disease of alcoholism. They're usually led by people who have many years in the program. MARILYN

Road Trip. When members of one group travel to visit and speak at a meeting of another group.

John D. Rockefeller. An early, nonalcoholic, supporter of A.A. In 1938, members of A.A., including BILL W. and DR. BOB, approached him hoping for a large donation to help them carry their message to alcoholics. Rockefeller wisely declined, fearing the professionalization of the program. Instead he donated $5,000, which supported Bill's and Dr. Bob's efforts for a year. In 1940 he held a dinner for many of his prominent friends, to introduce A.A. The dinner helped legitimize the floundering society. Rockefeller taught A.A. a valuable lesson; he spared his money, but gave of himself.

Rowland H. An early member of ALCOHOLICS ANONYMOUS. He was the man who visited Dr. CARL JUNG, as described in the BIG BOOK. Dr. Jung told him that he was a hopeless case. Rowland asked him if there were any chance for him. Jung replied yes, but only in the rare chance that he have a "vital spiritual experience." Rowland H. sought such an experience and connected with the OXFORD GROUPS. He helped EBBY T. sober up, an Ebby went on to tell BILL W. of his new life. Bill W. went on to be a cofounder of Alcoholics Anonymous.

Rude Awakening. Prerequisite to a spiritual awakening.

Rule 62. In 1940, an alcoholic who sobered up in A.A. proposed to create three corporations to promote the A.A. message, a club, a clinic, and a loan office. His plan contained sixty-one rules. He submitted it to A.A. headquarters in New York. Bill W. told him that other such plans had failed before, but that the man and his followers were welcome to ignore his warnings. They did ignore Bill's warnings, with disastrous results. Humbled, the promoter then mailed to every A.A. group in the United States a card. On the outside it read:

Group (the location) Alcoholics Anonymous
Rule 62

On the inside it said:

Don't take yourself too damned seriously.

S

St. Francis Prayer. See ELEVENTH STEP PRAYER.

Saint Louis, 1955. The second International CONVENTION of ALCOHOLICS ANONYMOUS. At this convention, Bill W., on behalf of A.A.'s OLD-TIMERS, turned the future care of the fellowship over to the GENERAL SERVICE CONFERENCE and its trustees.

St. Thomas Hospital. Akron, Ohio, hospital where DR. BOB and SISTER IGNACIA worked together to sober up some five thousand alcoholics. They medically treated and spiritually infused these sufferers.

San Diego, 1995. The most recent International CONVENTION of ALCOHOLICS ANONYMOUS. Celebrating A.A.'s sixtieth anniversary, the theme of this convention was "A.A. Everywhere, Anywhere."

Sanity. Seeing the world as it truly is, and reacting to it appropriately. *I like the analogy of peeling the layers of the onion. Addiction to drugs and alcohol was the top layer for me, relationship addiction is another, and food addiction is yet another. I'm striving to be the person that God intends me to be. There's a famous quote that talks about meeting St. Peter—he won't ask me if I was like Jesus, he'll ask me if I was the Tim God wanted me to be. I now realize that when I get in trouble, it's often my inner child reacting to fear and insecurity. The inner child takes control of my mind and body. The more I help that child to heal, the more I bring the child into accordance with my spiritual self, and we get closer to being one.* TIM

S-Anon. A 12-Step fellowship, modeled after AL-ANON, which helps members recover from the effects of being family or friend to a sex addict. The fellowship began in 1983 in Los Angeles, California, and now has 125 groups worldwide.

Saturday Evening Post. A JACK ALEXANDER piece about A.A. was the lead article in the March 1941 issue. Its positive reflection of the fellowship helped to bring in many new members. There were two thousand members at the start of 1941, and eight thousand by year's end. A.A. World Services publishes a pamphlet that reprints the article.

Henrietta Seiberling. Oxford Group member who introduced BILL W. and DR. BOB. She also went on to counsel families of alcoholics, and lend spiritual support to Dr. Bob and Bill.

Self-Centeredness. The state of always being concerned with one's own needs and desires. The Big Book describes this as the root of the addict's troubles. 12-Step programs provide the tools for recovering people to shift the focus off themselves, and onto serving God and other people.

Self-Debting. To spend too much time on the wrong thing, while not giving yourself what you really need, and just letting your needs go by. *I don't like the term because I think it's very important to be clear about what debting is—borrowing money that you can't pay back.* NICOLE

Selfish Program. People succeed in 12-Step recovery when they do it for themselves and not others, and when they go to any lengths to recover. Sometimes that means being selfish and saying no to the desires of others. Over time, when friends and relatives see an ADDICT's life change they begin to understand and appreciate the addict's selfishness. *Ted said to me, "If I lose you and the girls, I've lost everything." I grabbed hold of his tie and said, "You better go to treatment for yourself, not for the girls or me. There's no guarantee that I'll be here when you get back. I'll stay and run the business until you get back, and then we'll see."* MARILYN

Self-Knowledge. To understand your personal history, fears, desires, traits, tastes, strengths, and weaknesses. While self-knowledge enhances recovery, by itself it avails nothing.

Self-Supporting. A.A., and the programs modeled after it, do not accept contributions from sources outside the membership. Contributions from members pay the rent for the meeting place, and the cost of refreshments and literature. Groups generally send their surplus funds to help support area committees, intergroup offices, the General Service Office, and other service organizations within the fellowship. Members' contributions cannot exceed $1,000 per year. Declining outside contributions and limiting the contributions of members insure that no single source of income can wield too great an influence over the FELLOWSHIP.

Self-Will. What a 12-Stepper attempts to give up through the process of recovery. The Big Book says that any life run on self-will can hardly be a success. In the program, recovering people try to turn their will over to the care of a higher power—they try to do God's will, not their own.

Self-Will Run Riot. The BIG BOOK's great description of the life and behavior of an active ADDICT. Addicts tend to share more than their addictions—many share a tendency toward RESENTMENT and anger. Much of their trouble brews right out of themselves. They are self-centered and often in conflict with others.

Serenity. The state of being calm, quiet, and unruffled—no matter what life dishes out. *I have it when I have clarity. When my numbers are clear, even if I don't have enough money, I have serenity. I can't allow myself to be vague—if I don't know the facts, I get crazy. If I think there's a possibility I might debt, I call someone and that gives me serenity. If I don't call, even if I don't debt, I continue to think about it and I am not serene.* NICOLE

Serenity Prayer. The short, nondenominational prayer said at many 12-Step meetings. When BILL W. described seeing the prayer in an obituary, he said, "Never had we seen so much A.A. in so few words." In meetings, a shortened version of the original is said:

God Grant me the serenity to accept the things
I cannot change;
the courage to change the things I can; and the wisdom
to know the difference.

The long version goes on to say:

Living one day at a time; enjoying one moment at a time; accepting hardship as the pathway to peace.

Taking as He did, the sinful world as it is; not as I would have it.
Trusting that He will make things right if I surrender to His will.

That I may be reasonably happy in this life, and supremely happy with Him, forever in the next. Amen.

Service. Any action that helps CARRY THE MESSAGE of recovery to other ADDICTS. Many recovering people believe that personal recovery and serenity come through service to others. Service is vital in 12-Step programs, because the program's survival depends on the help of members, and members need the program to survive. *I found myself to be more comfortable in NA than I was in A.A. I also felt needed. NA was not as large a fellowship, so there was always something to do to help it grow. It seemed to be more exciting.* *MARY*

Seven Deadly Sins. As described in TWELVE STEPS AND TWELVE TRADITIONS' discussion of the Fourth Step, they are: anger, envy, gluttony, greed, lust, pride, and sloth.

Seventeen William Street. Newark, New Jersey, location of the first A.A. office, before the association took on the name ALCOHOLICS ANONYMOUS. BILL W. wrote most of the BIG BOOK in this small office.

Seventh Step Prayer. A short prayer that humbly asks God to remove personal shortcomings, as follows:

My Creator, I am now willing that you should have all of me, good and bad. I pray that you now remove from me every single defect of character which stands in the way of my usefulness to you and my fellows. Grant me strength, as I go out from here, to do your bidding. Amen.

Alcoholics Anonymous, page 76.
Reprinted by permission.

The Sixth and Seventh Steps came to get me. I was at the end of my rope—thoroughly miserable and discontent. People were talking about me then, the same as they did when I was drinking. I was out of control. I finally hurt enough that I began to look for relief. I found it in the Seventh Step prayer. I was in a hotel room, and I'd paid for three nights in advance and had thirty-nine cents in my pocket. I was trying to build a business and feeling like hell. I remember picking up the Big Book and reading the Seventh Step prayer. I had heard the words before, but I heard the message for the first time that night. It was as emotional an experience as the night that I admitted my powerlessness over alcohol. I realized that night that I was not only powerless over alcohol, but also powerless over everything in my life, so I prayed the Seventh Step prayer.
COOPER

Sex Addicts Anonymous. One of several 12-Step fellowships that help people recover from sex addiction. SAA began in 1977 in Minneapolis, Minnesota, and now has approximately five hundred groups worldwide.

Sexaholics Anonymous. One of several 12-Step fellowships that help people recover from sex addiction. SA began in 1981 in California, and now has approximately five hundred groups worldwide.

Sex and Love Addicts Anonymous. A 12-Step fellowship that helps members recover from addiction to sex, love, relationships, fantasy, romance, and codependency. The fellowship began in 1976 in Newton, Massachusetts, and now has approximately fifteen hundred groups worldwide.

Sexual Compulsives Anonymous. A 12-Step fellowship that is unique in their approach to recovery from sex addiction. Each member develops a personal recovery plan and defines sexual sobriety for themselves. Members then use the spiritual tools of the program and attempt to abstain from all behavior outside that plan. SCA was founded by gay men, and is mostly attended by gays and lesbians, but it is a program of recovery for men and women of all sexual orientations. The fellowship began in 1982 in New York City, and now has one hundred groups worldwide.

Shame. A painful emotion brought on by the consciousness of shortcomings or regrettable actions and feeling terrible about oneself as a result. It's the hole in the soul that many ADDICTS feel while active, and sometimes feel in recovery. Shame differs from guilt in that guilt says "I made a mistake," while shame says "I am a mistake." *As far back as I can remember, even before I started using, I had a huge sense of shame. I felt there was something fundamentally wrong with who I was. My escape from the shame was an attempt to create someone not myself—who others would like, be afraid of, or be intimidated by. The persona would be intentional, but not me. This was my shield from people getting to know me. I had a vague fear of being exposed. So I carried this huge shame. Using was a big part of it, but using became convenient because I could pinpoint it and blame it for my troubles. The shame coupled with desperation, knowing that I wasn't going to stop using.* *MARY*

Sharing. 1. Telling others about your EXPERIENCE, STRENGTH, AND HOPE in MEETINGS. 2. The interaction between two or more members of a 12-Step fellowship. *I heard around* *that many sponsors tell their newcomers not to share in meetings because they don't know anything. I asked my sponsor about that and he said, "Part of the problem we have as alcoholics is that we isolate. In recovery, we learn to share. It's important that you talk in meetings if you feel you have something to say."* COOPER

Dr. Samuel Shoemaker. An Episcopal cleric who headed the Oxford Groups in America at the time BILL W. joined that movement. He is the messenger from whom most of A.A.'s spiritual principles came. He helped Bill to see that prayer need not be an inventory of requests meant to influence the will of God, but that it could also be an exercise of listening for and hearing the will of God. According to Bill W., "Shoemaker passed on the spiritual keys by which we were liberated." Shoemaker had this to say about A.A.: "A.A. is one of the great signs of spiritual awakening in our time." And referring to spiritual awakening, Shoemaker said, "The basis of that belief was not theoretical, it was evidential. You could question the interpretation of the experience, but you couldn't question the experience itself. A.A. has been extremely wise in emphasizing the reality of the experience and acknowledging that it came from a higher power than man himself, and leaving the interpretation part pretty much at that."

Show Up, Do Your Best, Let Go of the Results. A plan for practicing the 12-Step principles in all your affairs.

Sick and Tired of Being Sick and Tired. A reason given by many recoverees for joining their 12-Step program.

Sick as Your Secrets. A slogan that encourages recoverees to be honest about everything. As long as secrets exist, shame exists, and shame can bring relapse. *In recovery, my bad behavior is gone, I've survived it. But the shame remains and I need to deal with it on a daily basis with honesty and* *sharing. The only remaining power is the secrecy, and that separates me from other people.* MARY

William Duncan Silkworth, M.D. The doctor at TOWNS HOSPITAL in New York City who treated BILL W. for alcoholism. He introduced Bill to the idea of alcoholism as an illness characterized by an obsession of the mind that condemns one to drink, and an allergy of the body that condemns one to die. At one time he told Lois, Bill's wife, that she had three choices: lock him up, watch him die, or watch him go insane. After Bill's spiritual conversion, Silkworth assured him he was not hallucinating and the change was real and worth holding on to. Dr. Silkworth wrote "The Doctor's Opinion" in the BIG BOOK. Bill called him "the little doctor who loved drunks."

Sister Ignacia. A nun who helped DR. BOB set up the country's first alcoholism unit at St. Thomas Hospital in Akron, Ohio. She worked there with Dr. Bob to care for, and bring the A.A. message to, over five thousand sufferers. After Dr. Bob's death, she continued her work at Charity Hospital in Cleveland. Assisted by members of local groups, she helped ten thousand more alcoholics find the A.A. message. When Dr. Bob and Sister Ignacia began their work together, the hospital frowned on the idea of treating alcoholics. So they bootlegged patients in under the disguised diagnosis of acute gastritis. They kept the worst patients in a room normally used for deceased patients awaiting the undertaker. They knew no one liked to go in there, so the drunks would go undetected.

Sitter. A person, usually a 12-Stepper, who stays with an ADDICT who is going through detoxification.

Slip. To go back to using the substances or behaviors of addiction. Slip is often used to mean a short relapse, with a quick return to the program. *I think there's a fine line*

between loving someone and taking care of someone, and it's real hard to define the line when you first get into recovery. The last slip I remember was at my dining room table, where many of my slips have taken place. When we were active, I'd put a meal on the table and call Ted to dinner. He'd come in and I would study his reaction to see if everything was OK. If I perceived it wasn't OK, I'd make my way back to the kitchen to try to figure out what was missing. The last slip I had was over something not being on the table. I caught myself saying, "What do you need?" to Ted. I did follow up well after I realized what I was doing by saying, "Whatever it is, you can get it yourself." Old habit patterns die hard. MARILYN

Do you know what an Al-Anon slip is? A moment of compassion. Overheard at an A.A. meeting.

SLIP. Acronym for Sobriety Lost Its Priority.

Smoke House. Term for an A.A. clubhouse, because of all the cigarette smoke.

SOB. Acronym for Sober Old Bastard. (Usually used with affection.)

SOBER. Acronym for Son Of a Bitch, Everything's Real.

Social Drinking. That elusive practice that most active alcoholics wish they could master. It means being able to take one or two drinks in the company of others, and then stopping. The allergy of the body of an alcoholic does not allow the person to stop. *Every Monday my parents would play bridge. So my friends and I would go to the shed and take a little out of this bottle and a little out of that bottle, so no one could tell we were taking it. We'd pour it all into one pint jar and come away with a concoction. It didn't matter to us because it all tasted like gasoline anyway, so mixing it was no problem. We might cut it slightly and* *then we'd just slam it down. This is what we called social drinking.* RON

Solitude. The state of being alone, or away from other people. Unlike ISOLATION, in recovery solitude is looked on as a positive practice. It is a time for reflection, PRAYER, MEDITATION, and strengthening the bond to a HIGHER POWER. One must be careful not to mistake solitude for isolation.

Spiritual Awakening. Becoming aware of a power greater than oneself. For some this happens in the form of a sudden, overwhelming God consciousness. For most, though, the awareness comes over time, as the result of practicing the 12 Steps. *I started to lose all our money. One day I knew we were almost broke and I had all my past to blame it on. I told my son I was going into my room for a while. I took some boards into the room, so I could nail myself in. I was seeing a psychiatrist and I stored up on some of the drugs she was giving me. I had a case of liquor too. I went in the room to die. I didn't come out for three days. The third day I woke up I took a board from the window and looked out and saw the moon. I had no idea what time or what day it was. I knew I'd been in the room for quite a long time because I had bed sores. I felt pretty bad and I looked pretty terrible. Seeing myself in the window enabled me to see myself and to step outside my body. This was such a gift. In my mind I was still this beautiful woman of dignity and honor—a woman of energy with a beautiful soul. God helped me that night because I saw the truth and I looked beyond myself as I looked at the moon. All of a sudden life didn't seem so dark, the room didn't seem so dark, life didn't seem so dark. I looked at the sores on my body, and I smelled the odor of the room. I looked up in the sky, then I looked back in the room. I had this moment of clarity. I looked at myself and said, "Audrey,* *you're a drunk, you're just a drunk." I looked at my life and realized that under all the facades and all the phoniness, I was just a drunk—nothing more, nothing less. Then I got scared and thought, Oh my God, what am I going to do? I tried to get up, but my legs wouldn't hold me. So I crawled. I tried to take one more swallow from a bottle. All of a sudden everything started to come out of me in projectile vomiting. I tried some pills, but nothing would stay down. I know now that that was God's intervening in my life.* AUDREY

I do have spirituality in my life, but it didn't happen overnight. This is a spiritual journey I am on. And I have a very strong conviction that it's a lifetime journey. RON

I've had one, as a result of the steps. It's been a process of letting go of myself. When you engage in reaching out to others, helping others, and see that we are all holding on to one another so no one falls out of the boat, it's hard not to see God in that. MARY

Spirituality. The state of being sensitive to, or attached to, a higher power. In a very broad manner, spirituality is the attraction to, and the appreciation of, the mysteries of life and matters of the soul.

Spiritual Program. The whole point of 12-Step programs is to help individuals find a power greater than themselves that will help them with their problem. DR. BOB put it this way: "There is no spiritual part of the A.A. program. A.A. is a spiritual program."

Spiritus Contra Spiritum. The formula for recovery that Carl Jung shared with Bill W. in their famous correspondence. Translated from Latin it means "God against booze."

Sponsee. A 12-Stepper who is helped along the spiritual journey by a more experienced member of the program. See SPONSOR.

Sponsor. A 12-Step group member who helps a member with less experience learn the program. In the beginning this may mean helping the newcomer find meetings and keep in contact with the program. The sponsor will guide the sponsee through the steps, and today is usually the person who hears the sponsee's Fifth Step. As time goes on and the sponsee finds comfort with the program and the steps, the sponsor becomes a trusted friend who helps the sponsee stay on the recovery path. *Back in 1966 when I came into A.A. there were only five or six meetings a week in my city (today there are over 160). Back then the old-timers kept track of me all the time. They'd call me here at the house to see why I missed a meeting. One guy would always call me about four in the afternoon because he knew my pattern and that's when I'd head for the post office and then to the bar.* TED

Early on I used sponsors. Now I co-sponsor with another guy, meaning we sponsor each other. JIM C.

Sponsorship really laid the foundation for my recovery. It was the first honest relationship I ever tried to have. I began learning to be who I am, and to be honest. The sponsorship relationship doesn't have the dynamics of other relationships, which gives you freedom to be honest in your learning. I learned how to be involved with another person without having to deal with the expectations of a friend or a partner. Sponsorship has been vital. Regardless of what goes on in other areas of my life, I make an effort to keep that relationship true and honest. If everything else goes to shit, I have to be honest with my sponsor. It also introduced me to the two-way dynamic. Before recovery, even when I had the best intentions, I'd use people. To some degree, everyone was a means to an end for me. To try to get away from that was a completely new experience. I learned to say, "This is who I am. Help me." I went into the sponsorship relationship knowing that I needed something, and that was OK for me and my sponsor. It was easier because I was supposed to be screwed up. I didn't have to look good, sound good, or know what was going on. That freedom did not exist in any other relationship. It's great not to have to waste a lot of time saving face. MARY

Step Meeting. A meeting where the topic for discussion is one of the 12 Steps. The meeting can be led off with a reading on the step, or by a member sharing their experience with the step.

Step Nazi (also Step Monster, Steppy). Humorous nickname for a sponsor who strongly encourages rigorous study of the 12 Steps, and always tells the sponsee that the solutions to problems are found in the 12 Steps.

Stepping Stones. The home of BILL and LOIS W. in Katonah, New York. Bill and Lois both lived there from 1941 until their deaths—Bill in 1971 and Lois in 1988. The home is now a museum and library run by the Stepping Stones Foundation, which Lois started to promote her husband's work. The home is open to visitors by appointment (call 914-232-4822).

STEPS. Acronym for Solutions To Every Problem, Sober.

Stick with the Winners. A suggestion to newcomers—that they hang out with people who work good programs and have a proven record of recovery.

Stinking Thinking. Addiction is the only disease which tells the sufferer that they do not have a disease. Any thoughts that promote this lie constitute stinking thinking. "I wasn't that bad," "maybe I can have just one," "what's the point anyway, I'll never be able to hold on," "people like me better when I drink"—these are all examples of stinking thinking.

Strength. 1. The God-given power to resist temptation. 2. The capacity for endurance. 3. A force as measured in numbers (as in a fellowship).

Suggested. The ingenious word placed before "program of recovery." Bill W. and the other pioneers thought they could help more alcoholics by saying the steps and experiences are offered as suggestions. They figured no alcoholic could rebel at a simple suggestion.

Suit Up and Show Up. A suggested way to live life when the recovering person is depressed, angry, fearful, or misguided. ADDICTS and CODEPENDENTS often have a long track record of hiding from life. This slogan means to simply be there and do the best you can in all situations. It's the 12-Step way to paraphrase Woody Allen's "ninety percent of life is just showing up."

Surrender. A key to recovery. In the Third Step, one makes a decision to turn one's life over to a higher power. In the Fifth Step, one abandons the need for secrecy and admits one's shortcomings to oneself, one's higher power, and to another person. In the Seventh Step, one relinquishes one's shortcomings to one's higher power. In the Eighth and Ninth Steps, one attempts to give up one's resentments by making amends to those who have been harmed. In the Twelfth Step, one abandons selfishness and makes an effort to help others. *When I finally surrendered, after struggling in the program and going in and out, I started going to a meeting every day. I also bugged my sponsor daily, asking, "When are we going to do the steps?" He told me* *that just by coming into A.A. I had already done the first three steps. He said, "You don't understand that yet, but let's get you started on your Fourth Step." Today my understanding of what my sponsor said is that by coming to A.A. I was coming somewhere for help because I couldn't help myself. I'd long known that I was powerless over alcohol, but now the unmanageability became the driving force. When I came in I didn't get the Second Step because I didn't see that I was insane. Now I know I'm insane. Step Three was my surrender, Uncle! Uncle! I give!* GREG

Sylvester. In one episode of the Warner Brothers cartoon series, Sylvester joins Birds Anonymous. He was 12-Stepped by another member, went to a meeting, got a few hours clean, and then was tempted. His sponsor tried to keep him off the feathers, but alas, Sylvester tried to do it his own way and wouldn't work the program. In trying to help Sylvester, the sponsor also relapsed. Lesson: it's easier for an active addict to get a recovering person to use than it is for a recovering person to get an addict clean.

T

Take What You Like and Leave the Rest. A suggestion used primarily in Al-Anon. People come into the programs with different backgrounds, different values, and different opinions. No one has to like or believe anything anyone else says. It's better to use what you find helpful in the program, and let others do the same. It can be tempting to abandon recovery just because of the opinions of a few, but this slogan helps people to focus on the good in others and find patience with the bad.

Taking Another's Inventory. The unhealthy practice of focusing on the shortcomings of another person. The programs suggest keeping the focus on oneself. Unfortunately, it's easier (and more fun) to keep another's inventory.

Taking a Tiger for a Walk. In programs such as A.A., GA, and NA, it's possible to practice complete abstinence from the addiction. But in OA complete avoidance of food is impossible. For newcomers, practicing moderation at mealtime is a difficult and tricky process which is likened to walking a tiger. It takes courage, strength, skill, and trust.

Telephobic. A person who is fearful or reluctant to use the telephone as a tool of recovery.

Telephone. An important tool of recovery. One cannot always be at a meeting, but a mini-meeting is always just a phone call away. When a recovering person reaches out to another for help, both benefit. The fellowships encourage new members to get plenty of phone numbers of group members, and to use them when they feel squirrelly or just want to talk to someone.

Telephonitis. A problem some recovering people have. They use the phone too much and drive their fellow recoverees crazy.

Tenth Step. The practice of taking one's inventory regularly, and admitting wrongs promptly. *One gift I've gotten from the program is an ability to see my mistakes, even as I am making them. Part of facing my character defects is getting to the point where I'm not afraid to see them. I no longer avert my eyes.*

When I'm having a nightmare, I can actually tell myself to wake up when it gets too intense. When I see myself practicing a character defect, I can let myself indulge in it until I say to myself, "OK, stop it." Then I can say to the other person, "I'm going in the wrong direction here, I need to back up." A lot of it is in doing things that are critical of others so that I can feel good about myself. I do it mostly in business dealings. But I can see when it's coming and actually back off, today. The most important part of the Tenth Step for me is not just admitting that I'm wrong, but promptly admitting it. I need to do it right then, before justification takes over and I tell myself that what I did wasn't that bad. COOPER

Terminal Uniqueness. Many active addicts and newly recovering people think that the program won't work for them because they are so different from other people. One of the powers of the program is that it works for anyone who thoroughly follows it. Believing you are unique and that it won't work can be deadly. *There were even times when I was little that I felt that God had made a mistake and I wasn't supposed to be here, but somewhere else. Nothing seemed to register. I didn't worry about the same things that others worried about.* COOPER

Terminal Vagueness. A term used in DEBTORS ANONYMOUS to describe the common symptom where many debtors spend money unconsciously, and then have nothing left to take care of their basic needs. *They say in DA that debtors suffer from terminal vagueness. That's true for me. I never knew how much money I had, I hardly ever had my checkbook balanced, I didn't know how much to put away for taxes. I always thought it was better to be artistic and creative and not worry about those details.* NICOLE

Think. A slogan that encourages 12-Steppers to think about the consequences if they want to use, and not just the momentary pleasure they might get. The "Think" sign is often turned upside down, relaying the message that recoverees' thought patterns have to be turned around if they are to stay on the right path. If a newcomer asks, "Why is that sign upside down?" he is told to "Think about it."

Third Step Prayer. A suggested prayer in the Big Book in which recoverees express a willingness to turn their will and life over to the care of their higher power. It reads as follows:

> God, I offer myself to Thee—to build with me and to do with me as Thou wilt. Relieve me of the bondage of self, that I may better do Thy will. Take away my difficulties, that victory over them may bear witness to those I would help of Thy Power, Thy Love, and Thy Way of life. May I do Thy will always!
>
> *Alcoholics Anonymous*, page 63.
> Reprinted by permission.

At treatment, after about twenty days, my counselor called me in and said, "Ted, we're not getting anywhere with you. Do you want to get well?" I said yes. "Well," she said, "will you be willing to do anything?" I said sure. She took out a little card she had in her desk with the Third Step prayer on it. She said, "I want you to take this card and go back to your room. Get on your knees and recite that prayer." I did, and it worked. TED

Thirteenth Step. The sexual pursuit of newcomers. It is practiced only by the sickest of group members. More spiritual members encourage newcomers to avoid all new relationships for the first year, and to keep the focus on recovery.

This Too Shall Pass. Slogan significant to newcomers experiencing withdrawal, and for everyone who is going through a tough time in recovery. It acknowledges that while life has its ups and downs, change is inevitable.

The Three A's of Recovery. *A*wareness of the disease, *A*cceptance of powerlessness over the disease, *A*ction of recovering through the program.

The Three C's or Al-Anon Recovery. I didn't Cause it, I can't Control it, and I can't Change it.

The Three Legacies of Alcoholics Anonymous. Unity, Recovery, and Service.

3-Step Program. A shortened version of the 12 Steps: Don't Drink, Trust God, and Clean House. Use the full twelve; you'll avoid loopholes.

To Keep It, Give It Away. Recovery can be compared to a body of water. If the water has an outlet, new water will flow in and the lake will remain clear and fresh. If the water is dammed up, new water cannot flow in and the lake becomes stagnant and murky. So it is with recovery. You must share your experience, strength, and hope with others to keep the energy of the spirit flowing into you, and through you. There's a story of BILL W. expressing dismay to his wife, Lois, that he had spent months trying to sober up other drunks, with no success. Lois said to him, "You've had plenty of success—you haven't drunk in six months!" *If you're trying to learn something, one good way is to teach it. I think that applies to this slogan. When I lead a GA meeting, I get to pick a topic, read about it, and pass it on. This gets the subject forefront in my mind and I learn more about it from others. JIM N.*

Tools of Recovery. The gifts you get upon entering recovery, if you are willing to use them. They are the ways that others have maintained their recovery, and include:

- Accept your powerlessness
- Air your emotions
- Ask God to remove your obsessions
- Avail yourself of a sponsor
- Avoid dependence on any one person
- Avoid loneliness

- Avoid major changes in the first year
- Avoid new relationships in the first year
- Avoid the first drink
- Be good to yourself
- Be mindful that addiction is cunning, baffling, powerful, and patient
- Change the routines of your life
- Change your friends
- Choose a home group
- Do the best you can and let go of the results
- Don't take yourself too seriously
- Eat a healthy diet
- Emulate others whom you admire
- Get needed rest
- Go to any lengths
- Go to meetings
- Hang out with other recovering people
- Keep an attitude of gratitude
- Keep away from mood-altering drugs
- Keep first things first
- Keep in mind that you have an incurable, progressive, and fatal disease
- Keep your anger in check
- Let go and let God
- Let others know the real you
- Listen
- Live in the day
- Meditate
- Practice rigorous honesty
- Practice the program one day at a time
- Pray
- Read program literature
- Recover for you, no one else

- Remain willing
- Remember it's a *we* program
- Remember that easy does it
- Remember your last use
- Remember: this too shall pass
- Stay active
- Stay away from drinking situations, unless there's a legitimate reason to be there
- Strive for balance
- Take inventory
- Talk out your resentments
- Thank God for another day
- Turn your will and life over to a higher power
- Use the telephone before you pick up the first drink or drug
- Watch for progress, not perfection
- When down, make a gratitude list
- Work with others

Towns Hospital. Facility in New York City where BILL W. went for his final treatment for alcoholism. He had recently met with EBBY T. and much of what Ebby had told him about God ran through his mind. Bill had his spiritual awakening at Towns Hospital. This is also where DR. WILLIAM SILKWORTH, who wrote "The Doctor's Opinion" in the BIG BOOK, worked.

Treatment Baby. A newcomer to 12-Step recovery, who has just come out of a rehab.

Trigger. A person, place, or thing that stimulates the obsession or compulsion of addiction. *It had started when I was eleven. A neighbor girl who was about six years older than me had seduced me. After that, no matter where we were, if we were alone, she and I would end up having sex. We* *had an affair for three years. The energy that took place then was very similar to what I experienced as an adult. It was a powerful, compelling, got-to-do-it sort of thing. So I stay away from women who trigger that feeling. It's like what we learn in OA about trigger foods. If I take a bite of a doughnut, I end up eating six doughnuts. If I eat a carrot, I eat one carrot. The women I avoid are like the trigger foods. I can have healthy sexual and romantic relationships, but not with any of the forbidden women.* JIM C.

I'm still developing my list of trigger foods. They are foods that for me start me on a binge and open up the flow inside. Obsessive thinking starts in me and I want to do the compulsive action of eating. Just like with drugs and alcohol, the more I use, the worse it gets. Simple sugars and fats are what I need to avoid. TIM

Trouble Shared Is Halved, Joy Shared Is Doubled. Saying that encourages 12-Steppers to talk about both pain and happiness with others.

Trust. Secure reliance on someone or something. 12-Steppers trust in a higher power, and often trust in one another.

Truth. The reality of life. Addicts spend most of their time running from the truth when active. They spend most of their time seeking the truth in recovery.

Walter Tunks. The Episcopal priest in AKRON, OHIO, who in the famous phone call BILL W. made from the MAYFLOWER HOTEL directed Bill to HENRIETTA SEIBERLING. She in turn helped Bill find DR. BOB.

Turn Over. To give your problems, worries, pain, fear, family, job, health, your entire life, to the care of a power outside yourself. For most turning something over is a process, which is aided by willingness and prayer.

Twelfth-Step Call. Visiting a suffering addict to bring the message of recovery. This work is best done in pairs—just as BILL W. and DR. BOB did with BILL D., A.A. member number three.

Twelfth-Step Work. Any act of service that helps carry the message of recovery. From setting up chairs at a meeting, to chairing an international convention; from giving a newcomer a ride to a meeting, to editing a program's magazine. Most commonly the term describes a recovering person trying to help an active addict find recovery. *There are people, and I'm not one of them, who can in just a few words firmly establish with a newcomer that they know what that person is going through. When they do that it makes the newcomers feel very welcome and gives them the feeling that they are in the right place. I can make a newcomer feel welcome and I go out of my way to do that, but I found out early on that I tend to try to sell the program to newcomers. That's not ideal. My sponsor, John, told me that many people carry the message to alcoholics by practicing the principles in all their affairs. This was a revelation to me. That's certainly the way John did it. John would tell me that he wasn't very good with newcomers, but at meetings, John was the person new people followed around. For me, I carry the message by going to meetings, by being active in A.A., and by tending the fellowship. I try to reach out to people who are sober but are having difficulties, or who just need someone to talk to. Taking care of the fellowship is important to me because the fellowship keeps me sober, along with my higher power. That's Twelfth-Step work for me. I love meetings where there are newcomers because they remind me that this thing works. I see myself in their eyes. But it's hard for me* *to get down there with them when they are in that shaky stage.* COOPER

Twelve Steps and Twelve Traditions. An A.A. conference-approved book, which studies each of the steps and traditions in detail. The steps are spiritual principles by which members try to live, and the traditions are guidelines for the unity and growth of the program. The book was written by BILL W., and was first printed in April 1953.

Twenty-Four-Hour Plan. The suggestion that an ADDICT break life down into one day. Can you stay clean for a day? If not, how about an hour? Addicts tend to concentrate on results. The twenty-four-hour plan allows them to concentrate on the job at hand.

U

Unconditional Love. Devotion and affection that are certain, under all circumstances. *I understand in the moments of conscious contact with God that God loves me unconditionally. It's hard for me to reach that understanding and keep it, but I know that it exists.* TIM

If I did something for my wife, I always expected something in return. Now I can do things for her for the simple pleasure of it, or for her benefit without expecting anything in return. It's the same with the people in GA. I offer myself and accept any risk or exposure that accompanies that, but I expect nothing in return. It's unconditional. JIM N.

Underearner. A phrase used in DA to describe a person who does not earn what they're worth. *An underearner is a debtor waiting to happen. Many people in DA are very talented, they just don't know how to ask for what they*

deserve. They seem unable to make enough to get ahead. NICOLE

Unique. Many people come to 12-Step recovery feeling that they are different from everyone else, and that the program won't work for them. If they stick around, they'll usually find they have much more in common with others than differences, and that the program can work for anyone no matter how special they are. See TERMINAL UNIQUENESS.

Unmanageable. A time in life when a person can no longer function successfully by means of the unaided will. For many this period goes on for years in active addiction, but denial keeps it from the awareness of the sufferer. *Toward the end of my active addiction, my recovering sister asked me if I thought my life was unmanageable. Well, I thought, mismanaged maybe, but not unmanageable.* RON

V–W

Victim or Volunteer? Saying that points out that addicts are victims of their disease until the day they find the means to recover. After that, they become volunteers to suffering.

Vote with Your Feet. All groups have their own style and quality. Some are hard-core, others laid back; some are restrained, others explore feelings. Recoverees vote for the meetings they prefer by walking into those meetings.

Walk the Walk. You can know the program through and through, and you can recite all the suggestions to others, but you don't find true recovery until you start to practice the principles in all your affairs.

The Way Out. A seriously considered title for the BIG BOOK. The AKRON group favored *Alcoholics Anonymous,* while the New York group liked *The Way Out.* Research at the Library of Congress ended the debate. Twelve books already had the title *The Way Out,* none carried the name *Alcoholics Anonymous,* so *Alcoholics Anonymous* it was. The alcoholics didn't want to be thirteenth at anything.

Wharf Rats. Groups of sober fans of the rock group The Grateful Dead. When the band was touring, the Wharf Rats gathered for meetings under an umbrella of yellow balloons during breaks in the concert. The name Wharf Rat comes from a Dead song of the same name, in which alcoholic August West tells his story. Wharf Rats have put a Grateful Dead twist on many of the familiar slogans. They call themselves "friends of August W.," and use such phrases as "one show at a time," "let go, let Jerry," and "another dopeless hope fiend."

Willingness. The key to recovery. Recovery in 12-Step programs takes work. Many are exposed to the recovery path, but only some decide to take it. The difference between those who recover and those who suffer in their addiction is the willingness to work and to change. Having the willingness to work the program is often the result of years of pain, and is a gift of God.

Wilson House. The birthplace of BILL W., and now an inn run by a nonprofit organization dedicated to preserving the memory of A.A.'s cofounder. There are fourteen rooms available, which can accommodate up to twenty-eight guests. Several A.A. and Al-Anon meetings are held each week in the meeting room and in the meeting house. For information write to The Wilson House, East Dorset, VT 05253; or call 802-362-5524. *When I visited the bed and breakfast it was a very spiritual experience for me. I guess it comes down to the feeling that I was at home. I tried to be there in the spirit of the moment. I had the opportunity to talk with another addict who was also visiting alone, and we made a connection. There was something there* *that made us want to continue to have a friendship. I believe in metaphysical connections, and the first night there I felt a presence in the rocking chair in my room. It was like times when I've felt another person in the room, I didn't hear them, but I turned around and they were there. It was a wonderful feeling of warmth and presence. After that, I'd sit and look at the chair and meditate.* TIM

Wilson's Drunks. Before ALCOHOLICS ANONYMOUS became autonomous from the OXFORD GROUPS, this was a nickname for the alcoholics who followed Bill W. The nickname was used with disdain by many nonalcoholic Oxfordians, and with humor and affection by the alcoholics themselves.

Window Hopping. A practice of many codependents who have not yet found recovery. It's the habit of going from window to window to see if the addict is on the way home. *I spent a lot of time window hopping when Ted was gone. I'd window hop all evening and when he finally did come home, I'd run up and jump in bed and pretend to be asleep.* MARILYN

Wisdom. Accumulated scientific or philosophic learning. The SERENITY PRAYER asks GOD to provide the wisdom to know the difference between what can be changed and what can't be changed. Wisdom comes from years of learning and practice, and that's why the wisdom of a 12-Step group is more trustworthy than the thoughts of any one member.

Withdrawal. 1. To undergo an often painful DETOXIFICATION from the drug of choice. 2. To hide from life and other people. The second definition may be less stressful, but it is dangerous. Many find that they cannot keep away from their addiction without the help and support of others.

Women's Groups. 12-Step groups designed to serve the special needs and concerns of women. Many women use these groups to address issues that they do not feel comfortable discussing in the presence of men. These groups can often give women a level of intimacy and fellowship they cannot achieve in mixed groups.

Workshops. Special, extended 12-Step MEETINGS in which participants work on specific recovery issues or steps. The Fourth Step is a big workshop topic. Often leaders will help participants do a searching and fearless moral inventory. Other topics include: relationships in recovery, any of the steps, women in recovery, letting go, meditation, and prayer.

X–Y–Z

YET. Acronym for You're Eligible Too.

Yets. All the things that might not have happened to an ADDICT—divorce, unemployment, mental wards, jail, death—but very well could have happened if the addict did not find recovery. *My alcoholism hasn't landed me in jail, yet. Overheard at an A.A. meeting.*

Zeal. Eagerness and spirited interest in the search for something. It's a recommended attribute for those pursuing 12-Step recovery.

Zero. What you get if you pursue the program with only partial effort.

Bibliography of Recovery Resources

Thousands of books, booklets, and pamphlets are published to help addicts recover. Here's a brief listing of the literature consulted in the writing of this book.

The A.A. Service Manual. Alcoholics Anonymous World Services, Inc., 1994. A guide to the service structure of A.A.

A.A. Tradition. How It Developed by Bill W. (pamphlet). Alcoholics Anonymous World Services, Inc. The history of the principles essential for A.A. unity and survival.

Al-Anon Faces Alcoholism. Al-Anon Family Group Headquarters, 1965, 1971, 1973, 1977, 1984. Al-Anon as viewed by the professional community, Al-Anon members, and the Al-Anon service structure.

"Alcoholics Anonymous" by Jack Alexander. The Curtis Publishing Company, 1941. An article about A.A. that appeared in *The Saturday Evening Post,* and propelled the growth of the A.A. program. Reprints available from A.A. World Services, Inc.

Alcoholics Anonymous. Alcoholics Anonymous World Services, Inc., 1939, 1955, 1976. The original book on 12-Step recovery, and still the most widely read.

Alcoholics Anonymous Comes of Age. Alcoholics Anonymous World Services, Inc., 1957, 1986. A brief history of A.A.

As Bill Sees It. Alcoholics Anonymous World Services, Inc., 1967. Collected abridged writings by Bill W.

Bill W. by Robert Thomsen. Popular Library, 1975. A biography of the cofounder of A.A.

Clancy Got Well by Jay R. Clancy. McGrevey Book Store, 1951.

Courage to Change. Al-Anon Family Group Headquarters, 1992. Daily meditations for Al-Anon members.

Dr. Bob and the Good Oldtimers. Alcoholics Anonymous World Services, Inc., 1980. A look at the contributions of Dr. Bob to A.A.

Further Along the Road Less Traveled by M. Scott Peck, M.D. Simon & Schuster, 1993. Edited lectures of the popular writer.

Grateful to Have Been There by Nell Wing. Parkside Publishing Corporation, 1992. Nell Wing's reminiscences of twenty years as executive secretary to Bill W., and seventeen more years as a close friend to Lois W.

Healing the Shame That Binds You by John Bradshaw. Health Communications, Inc., 1988. A study of one major cause of addiction, shame, and how to break free.

How Al-Anon Works for Families and Friends of Alcoholics. Al-Anon Family Group Headquarters, 1995. Helpful suggestions for living the Al-Anon way, and a collection of stories by Al-Anon members.

The Language of the Heart. The A.A. Grapevine, Inc., 1988. Bill W.'s *Grapevine* writings.

Living Sober. Alcoholics Anonymous World Services, Inc., 1975. A booklet filled with methods used by A.A. members to keep away from the first drink.

Narcotics Anonymous. Narcotics Anonymous World Service Office, 1984. The basic text of the NA program.

One A.A. member's story, written under a pseudonym.

The Recovery Book by Al J. Mooney, M.D., Arlene Eisenberg, Howard Eisenberg. Workman Publishing, 1992. Answers to the questions and concerns of recovering addicts.

The Road Less Traveled by M. Scott Peck, M.D. Simon & Schuster, 1978. A classic book about psychology and spiritual growth.

Touchstones. Hazelden, 1986. Daily meditations for men in recovery.

Twelve Steps and Twelve Traditions. Alcoholics Anonymous World Services, Inc., 1952, 1953, 1981. An in-depth study of each of the steps and traditions.

12-Step Program Contact Information

If you want more information about specific programs, please contact their service offices at the following addresses:

A.A. General Service Office
Box 459, Grand Central Station
New York, NY 10163

Adult Children of Alcoholics World Service Organization
P.O. Box 3216
Torrance, CA 90510

Adult Children of Dysfunctional Families
P.O. Box 462, Grand Central Station
Fond du Lac, WI 54935

Adult Children of Sexual Dysfunction
P.O. Box 8084, Lake Street Station
Minneapolis, MN 55408

Al-Anon Family Groups
1600 Corporate Landing Parkway
Virginia Beach, VA 23454

Alateen/Ala-Preteen/Alatot
1600 Corporate Landing Parkway
Virginia Beach, VA 23454

Alcoholics Victorious
1045 Swift Street
Kansas City, MO 64116-4127
E-mail: av@iugm.org

Augustine Fellowship—Sex and Love Addicts Anonymous
P.O. Box 119
Boston, MA 02258

Batterers Anonymous
8485 Tamarind Ave., Suite D
Fontana, CA 92335

Chemically Dependent Anonymous
P.O. Box 423
Severna Park, MD 21146

Children's and Youth Emotions Anonymous
P.O. Box 4245
St. Paul, MN 55104

Co-Anon Family Groups
P.O. Box 64742-66
Los Angeles, CA 90064

Cocaine Anonymous
9100 Sepulveda Blvd., Suite 216
Los Angeles, CA 90045

Codependents Anonymous
P.O. Box 33577
Phoenix, AZ 85067

Codependents of Sex Addicts
9337-B Katy Freeway, Ste. 142
Houston, TX 77024

Co-Sex and Love Addicts Anonymous
P.O. Box 614
Brookline, MA 02146

Debtors Anonymous
P.O. Box 400, Grand Central Station
New York, NY 10163

Depressed Anonymous
1013 Wagner Ave.
Louisville, KY 40217

Dual Disorders Anonymous
P.O. Box 4045
Des Plaines, IL 60016

Emotional Health Anonymous
P.O. Box 429
Glendale, CA 91202

Emotions Anonymous
P.O. Box 4245
St. Paul, MN 55104

Families Anonymous
P.O. Box 3475
Culver City, CA 90231

Food Addicts Anonymous
P.O. Box 057394
West Palm Beach, FL 33405

Gam-Anon Family Groups
P.O. Box 157
Whitestone, NY 11357

Gamblers Anonymous
3255 Wilshire Blvd., Suite 610
Los Angeles, CA 90010

Impotents Anonymous and Al-Anon
P.O. Box 5299
Maryville, TN 37802

Incest Survivors Anonymous
P.O. Box 17245
Long Beach, CA 90807

Isolators Anonymous
130 W. 75th St.
New York, NY 10023

Marijuana Anonymous
P.O. Box 2912
Van Nuys, CA 91404

Mental Illness Anonymous
1895 Laurel Ave.
St. Paul, MN 55106

Nar-Anon Family Groups/Narateen
P.O. Box 2562
Palos Verdes, CA 90274

Narcotics Anonymous
P.O. Box 9999
Van Nuys, CA 91409

Neurotics Anonymous
11140 Bainbridge Dr.
Little Rock, AR 72212

O-Anon (families and friends of compulsive overeaters)
P.O. Box 748
San Pedro, CA 90733

Obsessive-Compulsive Anonymous
P.O. Box 215
New Hyde Park, NY 11040

Overeaters Anonymous
P.O. Box 92870
Los Angeles, CA 90009

Pill Addicts Anonymous
P.O. Box 278
Reading, PA 19603

Recovering Couples Anonymous
World Service Organization

P.O. Box 11872
St. Louis, MO 63105

S-Anon (families and friends of sex addicts)
P.O. Box 5117
Sherman Oaks, CA 91413

Schizophrenics Anonymous
15920 W. Twelve Mile
Southfield, MI 48076

Sex Addicts Anonymous
P.O. Box 70949
Houston, TX 77270

Sexaholics Anonymous
P.O. Box 300
Simi Valley, CA 93062

Sexual Compulsives Anonymous
P.O. Box 1585, Old Chelsea Station
New York, NY 10011
E-mail: info@sca-recovery.org

On the Internet

More and more information about 12-Step recovery appears on the Internet every day. The following sites and meetings will get you started on the path to cybriety.

Sites

A.A. Intergroup and Central Office Phone Numbers

http://www.moscow.com/Resources/SelfHelp/AA/phone/phone.html

A worldwide listing of local A.A. service centers.

A.A. Meetings Online

http://www.crl.com/~pac/aa/

A directory of meeting and other A.A. resources online.

Adult Children Online Resource Page

http://www.intac.com/%7Ewoy/drwoititz/source.htm

A listing of information and resources relating to alcoholism and other dysfunctional life-related issues.

Al-Anon and Alateen

http://solar.rtd.utk.edu/~al-anon/

Includes a statement of what Al-Anon is and what it is not, a questionnaire to help determine if Al-Anon or Alateen is for you, *Twelve Steps and Twelve Traditions,* and a world-wide listing of how to get in touch with Al-Anon and Alateen.

Alcoholics Anonymous

http://www.alcoholics-anonymous.org/index.html

A Web page created and maintained by A.A. World Services, Inc.

Available in English, Spanish, and French.

Includes an A.A. fact file, and a listing of international general service offices.

***Alcoholics Anonymous* (the Big Book)**

http://uts.cc.utexas.edu/~clyde/BillW/BB_Introduction.html

This version includes the Forewords, "The Doctor's Opinion," Chapters One through Eleven and Appendix II. Unfortunately, the personal stories of recovering people are not included.

Alcoholics Anonymous Information

http://www.csic.com/aa/index.html

Includes a bookstore of recovery titles, and ordering instructions.

Personal stories of several A.A. members.

Information about A.A. in a well-laid-out question and answer format. And a listing of myths and truths about alcoholism and A.A.

Cocaine Anonymous

http://www.ca.org/

A self-test for addiction, and U.S. and international infoline phone numbers.

Courage to Change Catalog

http://www.courage.com/ctc.html

A recovery bookstore on the Net. Many books on addiction, recovery, and other life challenges are available to order direct.

The History of Lip Balm Anonymous
http://guide-p.infoseek.com/Titles?qt=alcoholics+anonymous&col=WW&st=40&sv=N2&lk=noframes
Great spoof of a recovery home page.

A Journey to Recovery (from a member of OA)
http://www.geocities.com/TheTropics/2061/
An eating plan and other literature, Web recovery resources, Web catalogs.

Keep It Green Recovery Page
http://www.heartlink.com/green.htm
A listing of literature, links, and information.

Lamplighters
http://www.commspec.com/resources/lls.htm
Home page of an online A.A. group.

Narcotics Anonymous
http://www.crl.com/~nike/rec/na/index.html
Includes literature, and links to area and regional Web sites, NA online meetings, and news groups.

The Phoenix
http://137.192.243.21/phoenix/
Web page of the monthly recovery newspaper. Web page allows access to the newspaper's archives. Subscription info also available.

Recovery Anonymous
http://www.mlode.com/~ra/index.html
Advocates steps beyond the 12 Steps, to find "who we were meant to be."

Self-Help and Psychology Magazine
http://www.well.com/user/selfhelp/
An online magazine for recovering and other enlightened people.

Sexual Compulsives Anonymous
http://www.sca-recovery.org/

Includes literature, information on how to find an SCA meeting, getting in touch with SCA, and an SCA calendar.

Sobriety and Recovery Resources

http://www.winternet.com/~terrym/sobriety.html

A comprehensive listing of recovery resources, as well as personal stories, A.A. links, other program links, commercial resources, humor, E-mail support and feedback, recovery and support news groups.

USA Recovery from Debt Home Page

http://www.voicenet.com/~blowry/debt.html#
Twelve_step_resources

Includes information on Debtors Anonymous and other organizations and resources that will assist compulsive debtors.

OnLine 12-Step Meetings

Chapter Seven's Men

Contact: mailto:baritone@cts.com

Cybriety (Women's Group)

Contact: ClaireW@pluto.njcc.com

Cybriety2 (Women's Group)

Contact: Frenchabby@aol.com

Lamplighters (A.A.)

Contact: lls-approval@world.std.com

Meeting of the Minds (A.A.)

Contact: MOM-L-Request@SJUVM.STJOHNS.EDU

REBELLION DOGS

Contact: linmu@teleport.com

RecoverEmail Group an ALL Fellowship 12 Step Group

Contact: recovery@usal.com

Trudgers (Big Book study)

Contact: trudgers-request@bga.com

Acknowledgments

Thanks to Steve Silberman and David Schenk for their book *Skeleton Key: A Dictionary for Deadheads.* Their book inspired the idea for this book.

Thanks to my wife, Gail, who put up with loneliness during evenings and weekends, and raised our beautiful daughter, Maggie, while I researched and wrote.

Thanks to all the contributors, some of whom are now very good friends. They helped me to see the true power of the program comes from God working through other people. I now believe as I never did before.

Thanks to Bruce Tracy, the editor who believed in this project from the beginning; and to Eliza Truitt, who helped me through the final editing stages.

About the Author

Christopher Cavanaugh is a veteran of the publishing industry. He was an editor at *Family Circle* in New York City, as well as the managing editor for Meredith Books in Des Moines, Iowa. He is currently managing editor for Reader's Digest General Books. He lives in New York.